Hillary's Kitchen

Dietary Feeds for Dietary Needs

The Guide to Healing the Body with Food as The Medicine

Hillary Teske,

B.S. in Culinary Nutrition

Magna Cum Laude

Disclaimer: Based on my education, I did quite a bit of research for this project and have included outside sources. All my recipes (including ingredients) may help improve, reduce, or prevent an illness, disease, or chronic pain.

Published in the United States By: Amazon Kindle Direct Publishing

This picture was taken at the Bear Creek Greenbelt Park in Lakewood, CO.

Then God said, 'Behold, I have given you every plant yielding seed that is on the surface of all the earth, and every tree which has fruit yielding seed; it shall be food for you."

~ Genesis 1: 29

This scripture above explains that we have many resources right at our hands. We must learn how to use these plants, seeds, fruits, grains, and meats in the most nutritious and delicious way to satisfy and heal our bodies, minds, and cravings.

Contents

Dedication

This book is dedicated to my parents, Shelby Brian and Nancy L Harris. Thank you for all the love and support you gave me as I was growing up. I pray you can see me and be a part of my life from our Lord's Kingdom.

Acknowledgments

Every disease/illness I discuss in my cookbook I have experienced in my life. I have not experienced them personally. However, someone in my family has, so I have seen these illnesses firsthand. I also completed a nutrition internship at an eating recovery center, so I have seen how eating discords change people through my work as well. At the eating recovery center for my nutrition internship, I learned that the disease could be very misleading and felt it was important to shed some light on the subject.

I strive to help and educate the most people about these illnesses, so we all can live our best lives. I would like to thank my husband Kenton Teske for all the picture taking and support he has given me towards this book. He even came up with part of the title "Dietary Feeds for Dietary Needs." I would like to thank everyone that was a part of my education related to both nutrition and culinary. I am very thankful to all my friends and family as well, that helped inspire my first cookbook.

Food is not solely for surviving. Yes, food allows your body and mind to function properly. However, I would encourage you to pay attention to how food makes you feel both emotionally and physically. In most cultures' food is also particularly important with embracing who they are as individuals, as a community, and as a family. It is important to embrace food, where it comes from, what it does in your body, and that it truly makes you happy. Food is a way of life while showing the world who you are through food, and lastly, enjoying time with friends and family.

Food Heals the Body and Mind!

Who's Behind Hillary's Kitchen?

Hillary (Harris) Teske's Story

Hillary grew up in the beautiful valley of Grand Junction, Colorado. Growing up, she loved to put her energy into the kitchen and has always had a passion for cooking and experimenting with new recipes. As Hillary grew older, she realized that her love was not only for cooking; she wanted to help people through food and nutrition.

After Hillary graduated High School, she attended Johnson & Wales University, Denver Campus. Hillary obtained an Associate in Culinary Arts (2020) and a Bachelor's in Culinary Nutrition with a minor in Professional Communication (2021). Throughout college, she grew an appreciation for writing and how food helps heal the body. During College, Hillary worked at Denver Health as a food service worker and then as a cook intern. She was trained in the entire food service and nutrition department and gained experience regarding diet regulations, cooking skills, and leadership. Hillary then completed her nutrition internship at the Eating Recovery Center in Denver, Colorado. Throughout the training, she prepared and cooked meals to precise measurements and plating techniques for the patients.

When Hillary graduated from college, she moved back to Grand Junction and married her love. Hillary is currently working at Devils Kitchen/Hotel Maverick as a Line Cook/Barista Supervisor. While working at Devils Kitchen, she developed this educational cookbook. Hillary hopes this book helps educate people about foods and recipes that can help prevent, help heal or help manage an illness in the body.

Food is not solely for surviving. Food is a way of embracing who you are and who you want to be while living a long, happy, healthy life. Food heals the body.

Fun Facts About Me

My husband Kenton and I are big Foodies. We love trying new food/restaurants and watching food competitions on TV. We also love going on outdoor adventures with our dogs, Athena and Freya.

How Food Changed My Perspective

Part One

I believe my passion for cooking started in my grandma's kitchen. Growing up, I remember my grandma making sure my family and I always had food to eat and questioning why we did not always eat breakfast. I can still envision the inviting smell of sausage in the morning and the crisp taste of cucumbers in the afternoon.

My parents and I traveled to Missouri from Colorado to visit my grandparents every year. While there, my grandma sometimes made sausage gravy from scratch to pour over buttery biscuits for breakfast. We then had a salad with cucumbers and tomatoes later in the day to go with dinner.

We always had a large family gathering with food when we visited. My parents and I stayed with my grandparents, so I was able to help my grandma in the kitchen. I would help her make the nacho cheese sauce, deviled eggs, veggie trays, and more. My grandma then pulled out her recipe cards and spread them all over the counter to find the two- family favorite ice cream recipes. Homemade Ice Cream is a staple at all family gatherings. We would make a version with sweetened condensed milk and standard vanilla ice cream. I loved both recipes as a kid, and I still do today.

While we were finding the recipes and mixing up the ingredients, my dad and grandpa would go to the store to buy several bags of ice and rock salt (two essential elements to freeze the ice cream while it turns). After the ingredients were mixed, I poured the mixture into the ice cream machine (a tall metal cylinder container). I brought the container outside into the garage and placed it into the wooden bucket. My dad then attached the motor to the container. Lastly, my grandpa put rock salt and ice cubes around the outside of the container and turned on the machine. Making ice cream with ice and salt could get messy, so it was always best to be made outside. As the cream turned, I remembered the annoying grinding sound of the ice and salt between the metal container and the wooden bucket. However, the sound was always worth that sweet and delicate taste of ice cream. Homemade ice cream is always the show and a great way to end the family gathering. When my parents and I headed back to Colorado, sometimes I would take recipes that my grandma wrote down to cook at home.

Of course, one of my favorite recipes she ever gave me was both of her ice cream recipes, following the leftover Thanksgiving Turkey Noodle Casserole recipe. The casserole includes thick egg noodles with plenty of leftover turkey meat veggie broth seasoned with poultry seasoning, salt, and pepper. A great thing about this dish is that you can taste every component and ingredient throughout the casserole. It may seem simple, but trust me. It is a great way to use your leftover turkey both simplistically and deliciously.

Part Two

Growing up, I would choose new recipes to cook every week and go grocery shopping with my mom. I can remember the first time I made fresh pasta from scratch. *(See pages 112- 113 for the recipe)* I had sheets of pasta across the kitchen counters and flour everywhere! Once the fresh noodles were cut to shape and cooked, I lightly tossed them in a buttery garlic and herb sauce and served them alongside steak and veggies. The fresh pasta was very inviting and tasted swell. It was intriguing to me to create my dish from simple ingredients that you could buy at a local grocery store or a farmer's market. The very idea of cooking for people brought me joy. "My mom always told me, "People will always need to eat, so you can easily make a career out of it." So, when I graduated high school, I decided to go to Culinary School.

I can remember my first days of school, getting dressed in my chef whites and putting my knife bag over my shoulder while walking to class. I was so excited! In school, we learned all types of cooking, from the fundamentals to different cuisines. Some days were hard and embarrassing when the chef instructor yelled at you or other students for messing up. There were also amazing days when the chef told you, "This is the best chili I've had from a student in a while." The chefs' criticism made me stronger and more independent as a cook and leader. During college, I worked at a few local food establishments and in a couple of healthcare kitchens. I decided I wanted to do more with my life than just work in a kitchen. I love the drive of cooking at a fast pace while completing orders for customers; it brings chills up my spine and into my heart, But I know I can do more than just cook for people and make them happy. I can also help heal people through food and nutrition.

When my father passed away, my world stopped. As I was grieving and coping with my loss, I put all my energy into the lord, my education, my career, and my fiancé (now husband). I realized my purpose from God is more significant than just cooking for people. My goal is to help give people information on maintaining or preventing their bodies from an illness or disease with food as medicine.

Cooking and the Culinary Industry will always be my passion! I will always prepare food for my family and friends to eat that gives them those nostalgic memories, just as my grandma did when I was young. My goal is to use my passion for culinary while combining my skills and knowledge of food and nutrition to help others. Food heals the body.

Current Food Trends

We all know that the COVID-19 Pandemic has had tremendous negative impacts on people's mental health. I am here to tell you; that it is predicted in 2022 and the next five years. People will want to reduce all health risks as the pandemic fades and people get back to "normal" living and gathering.

In global food and drink trends, people want to feed their minds, experience quality redefined meals, and become united by food.

Image Credit: (Cap Wellness Center, 2022)

Feed Their Mind: now that the pandemic is fading, it is discussed that people around the globe want to make a change and take control of their lives and health. Thus, the food industry will start to form brands and products that will help with healthy eating for the mind. Jenny Zegler, associate director of Mintel Food and Drink, said. "We predict that innovative food and drink formulations will help people learn how diet can impact mental and emotional health, which will lead to new interest in psychology-based approaches to healthy eating" (Mintel Group, 2021). The public wants control after over a year of having un- knows. The best way to take control is to help yourself and your loved ones when it comes to one's health and healing the body with food.

Quality Redefined: The next trend that the world is looking at is upscale meals for at-home entertainment. Experts believe people will want to celebrate more with exclusive at-home meals than going out. With this, people will either be getting their events catered or need access to easy-reading upscale and healthy cookbooks. The Mintel Group talks about how consumers will want to get the most bang for their buck when shopping for groceries and in-home items. This does not just involve the price; it also involves ethical and environmentally friendly things. Consumers will also be looking for convenient and adventurous items in a hygienic food service establishment. Even though the pandemic is ending, the public will still expect regular cleaning in restaurants and markets.

Over the years, people have become increasingly aware of how companies treat their employees and how goods and services are made and provided. When people are observant and only purchase items from ethical and environmentally friendly companies, this helps improve your carbon footprint and the employee's mental health, and your own. Companies that have unethical practices hinder their employees' mental and environmental health. This results in the trend of buying and producing sustainable products.

United by Food: Food services and mental health companies will encourage consumers to use their current and new brands to express themselves as the person they are or want to become. Expressing yourself through these goods and services is a way to connect with your pre-pandemic self and regain control of your life's mental and physical health through food, clothes, activities, and more. As companies adapt their brands to the new needs of communities, they will be giving back and helping people overcome the tragedies that the pandemic has caused. "Consumers' understanding of the community has been strengthened by COVID-19," Zegler said. "Recognizing the importance of connection and support, consumers will organize in like-minded communities for socialization and camaraderie" (Mintel Group, 2021). Similar food and drink brands can bring communities together and make a difference in today's "new" society, figuring out the "new" normal of the after-pandemic effects.

The food and health trends that I have discussed above prove that it is more important than ever for the food and mental health industries to come together. The pandemic has caused depression, anxiety, and stress of the un-know. Now that the pandemic is fading, these industries are coming together to help the world with mental health and healthy eating and living. The trends above suggest that people want help and want to take control of their lives through healthy cooking and living to reduce stress and improve their overall health. I am so excited about these new trends, and I pray they help people with mental and physical health. Food heals the body.

The Three Sisters

The magic behind the ancient Native American farming method

We as people need guidance from family, friends, teachers, and role models to help us grow as individuals. Plants need the same support system to grow as well.

Many native American communities believe that the three sisters of seeds (corn, beans, and squash) are some of the most essential crops you can plant. When you grow the three sisters together, they thrive off each other. Thus, these three sisters are a big part of the Native American culture and culinary traditions.

How it Works:

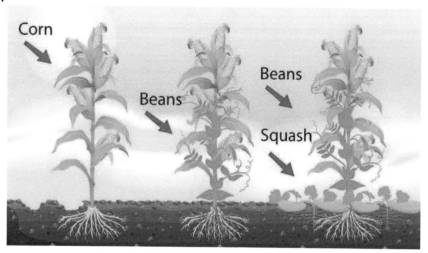

Image Credit: Badaczewski, L. (2020, December 14)

Beans: Receive shade from the squash leaves so the beans do not dry out from the sun. In return, the beans provide nutrients (natural plant food) to the squash and corn.

Corn: Provides a natural pole for the beans to vine up. The beans then stabilize the corn stalks from blowing over in the wind.

Squash: Traps moisture in the soil. This trapped moisture helps the three sisters grow in dry climates. The squash also provides a living mulch from their shallow-rooted vines.

Whole & Ground Spices With a Few Oats

Tips Before You Start Cooking

o **Mise En Place**
  - o A French term in the culinary world that translates to "putting in place."
  - o "Putting in place" is a good practice to use in your everyday life and, of course,
    when you are in the kitchen. Mise en place refers to getting all your prep done before starting a task.
    - ▪ When looking at a recipe, take out all the equipment and ingredients needed. Next, prep (measuring & cutting) all the veggies, grains, spices, and liquids before cooking. This will speed up the cooking process and result in a smooth and less stressful time in the kitchen.

o **Toasting Whole or Ground Spices**
  - o ***Flavor:*** You might wonder how they can achieve such divine taste in a dish when you are at a restaurant. It all has to do with the cooking technique, the quality of the ingredients, and the "life" of the spices.
  - o ***Life Of the Spice:*** The most robust flavor of spices only lasts for six months. After the six months are up, the flavor has declined drastically. I keep my spices for 1 to 2 years at the very most in my kitchen. Anything older than that is best just to throw out.
  - o ***Toasting:*** Whether your spices are brand new or a year old, the best ways to gain the most flavor are to one, use whole spices and two, toast your spices before adding them to a dish.
    - ▪ You can toast both whole and ground spices in a dry pan on the stove.
    - ▪ <u>Hint</u>: Toasting gives the same enhanced flavor to raw nuts/seeds and uncooked grains.

Directions:

1. Place a small pan on the stove over medium heat and add the spices. *(Toast each spice separately so that you can quickly grind and measure the spices individually. If you are using pre-ground spices, measure out all the spices you need for a specific item and toast them together.)*
2. Toast the spices over medium heat for 2-4 minutes.
3. Stir occasionally, and do not walk away, or your spices might burn.
4. When you start smelling, the spices come to life, remove the spices from the pan and place them in a bowl to stop cooking. Once the spice has cooled slightly, you can grind them/add them to your dish.

- **Grinding Whole Spices**
  - You gain the most flavor from freshly ground whole spices. As they are crushed, the spices release their natural aromatics and oils. Ground spices can sit on a shelf for six months; the aromatics and flavor will fade after that.
  - I would highly recommend investing in whole spices and a spice grinder.
    - *Hint*: Whole spices will also last longer on your shelf than ground spices.
- **Taste As You Are Cooking**
  - Some factors will change the results of your dish. These factors may include the size/quantity of the food item, the quality of the ingredients, or the altitude you are located at. It is best to taste throughout the cooking process to adjust seasoning and liquids that may or may not be required.
- **What is Super Food?**
  - A food item that is exceptionally high in antioxidants or other nutritional properties is known to improve one's health.
- **Terms:**
  - *Chiffonade: Roll the leaves into a "tube" and cut them into thin strips.*
  - *Cut On a Bias:* This term can mean cutting against the grain when referring to meat. And when referring to vegetables, it can mean to cut at a 45-degree angle *(cut diagonally instead of straight down).*

Veggie/Chicken Broth

Commonly Used Broths & Sauces in My House

Vegetable Broth
- o Benefits of Making Your Broth:
    - When you buy meat and veggies from the store, you pay by weight. Most people might not think much of carrot peels or chicken bones as money wasted. But after a while, those peels and bones add up.
    - In the long run, you are saving money by making your broth with products you already have in the house that you might normally throw away.
    - Making your broth is more environmentally friendly because you are not wasting packing that store-bought broth comes in.
    - Using broth instead of water is a nutrient booster for your dish.
    - Lastly, you can control the ingredients—specifically sodium levels and no additives.
        - I do not salt my broth because you never know what dish you will end up using the broth for. You do not want to risk a dish being too salty.
    - After you make the broth, you can keep it in a sealed container for up to 1 week in the fridge. Or up to 3 months in the freezer.
    - **Yield:** 4 cups (32oz)

Ingredients:

1 Onion roughly chopped.
- Onion scraps

1 Leek bulb/end of leek you usually throw away.
2 large Carrots roughly chopped.
- Carrot peels

2 Celery stalks roughly chopped.
- Ends of Celery/Scraps.

½ cup Washed Potato Skins. Dirty potato skins can result in a cloudy broth.
4-5 cups of Water

Other
Any veggie scraps you have/produce, save for the broth.
No mushrooms, leafy greens, cabbage, broccoli, or brussels sprouts. These veggies can result in a bitter broth.

Aromatics
4 Bay leaves
1 Tablespoon Tri-Colored Pepper Corn
1 Bunch of Fresh thyme, leaves, stems, and all
1 Bunch of Fresh parsley, leaves, stems, and all

Directions:

1. Place all vegetables and scraps in a large pot.
2. Add in aromatics and water.
3. Bring to a bowl, then reduce to a light simmer. Cover with a lid and let simmer for at least 5 hours. The longer you cook the broth, the better the flavor will develop.
4. Once the broth has simmered to your liking, strain the broth into a container or pitcher. Discard all veggies, scraps, and aromatics.
5. Allow the broth to cool completely before covering the container with a lid. You can place the container of broth in the fridge and stir every hour until the broth is cold. Or set the container in an ice bath on your counter and do the same thing. Once the broth is complexly cooled, place the lid on and store it in the refrigerator.

Chicken Broth

Ingredients:

1 Onion roughly chopped.
- Onion scraps

2 Carrots roughly chopped.
- Carrot peels/ends

2 Celery stalks roughly chopped.
- Celery ends/scraps

Chicken-Bones *leftover from chicken wings or a whole chicken carcass/scrap of unwanted meat. You can also make a turkey broth around the holidays with turkey bones/scraps.*

4-5 cups Water

Other

Any other veggie scraps you have that are appropriate for broths.

Aromatics
4 Bay leaves
1 Tablespoon Tri-Colored Pepper Corn
1 Bunch Fresh thyme, leaves, stems, and all
1 Bunch Fresh parsley, leaves, stems, and all

Directions:

1. Place all vegetables and scraps in a large pot.
2. Add in chicken bones, aromatics, and water.
3. Bring to a bowl, then reduce to a light simmer. Cover with a lid and let simmer for at least 5 hours. The longer you cook the broth, the better the flavor will develop.
4. Once the broth has simmered to your liking, strain the broth into a container or pitcher. Discard all bones, veggies, scraps, and aromatics.
5. Allow the broth to cool completely before covering the container with a lid. You can place the container of broth in the fridge and stir every hour until the broth is cold. Or set the container in an ice bath on your counter and do the same thing. Once the broth is complexly cooled, place the lid on and store it in the refrigerator.

Tomato/Pizza/Spaghetti Sauce

- Making your spaghetti sauce is the best way to control the ingredients. When you buy sauce at the store, there will likely be preservatives, sugar, and other non-wanted ingredients. You can add veggies and customize the flavor for a tasty and nutritious sauce when making your own.
- This sauce is a great way to use tomatoes from your summer garden.
- Tomatoes: Full of antioxidants and are low in carbs while having welcoming health benefits. Adding tomatoes to your diet may provide anti-inflammatory properties in your body (heart-healthy). These anti-inflammatory properties can be incredibly beneficial to overall mental and physical health.
- Carrots: Everyone knows carrots are good for your eyes! So, I would like to provide you with some more health benefits. They are low on glycemic index levels (how fast a food races your blood sugars) and contain fiber, biotin, and more. Biotin helps improve your fat and protein metabolism.

- **Yield:** 4-6 Cups

Ingredients:

2 Tablespoons Olive oil
1, 32oz can Diced Tomatoes (juices and all) or Fresh Tomatoes
1 small to medium yellow onion, small dice
1 large carrot, small dice
2 Celery Stalks, small dice
½ Green Bell Pepper, small dice
4oz Fresh Mushrooms, small dice
3 Fresh Garlic Cloves, minced
½ teaspoon Dried thyme leaves
½ teaspoon Dried Oregano
½ teaspoon Red Pepper Flakes
½ teaspoon Salt
¼ teaspoon Pepper
1 teaspoon Granulated Sugar

Garnish
½ bunch Basil, chiffonade

Directions:

1. Fresh Tomatoes: Bring a pot of water to a simmer, big enough for the tomatoes.
2. Score the bottom of the tomatoes and make an X. Scoring the tomatoes now will be easier to peel them later.
3. Simmer the tomatoes in the water until you see the skin start and peel away/shrivel.
4. Remove tomatoes and allow them to cool slightly. Once the tomatoes are cool enough for you to handle, peel off all the skin.
5. Remove the core of the tomatoes and place it in a food processor or blender. Puree until smooth.
6. Using Canned Tomatoes, Start Here: Place a large pot over medium to high heat. Add in the olive oil and all the veggies. Sautee for 5 minutes or until the veggies are completely soft/translucent. Stir occasionally.
7. Add garlic, thyme, oregano, sugar, red pepper flakes, and salt/pepper. Sautee for another 1-2 minutes.
8. Add in the fresh pureed or canned tomatoes and stir.
9. Cover the pot and simmer for 20-30 minutes.
10. Taste and adjust seasoning.
11. If the sauce is too thick, add hot vegetable broth or water.
12. If you desire a smooth tomato sauce, you can use a blender or immersion blender to puree the tomato sauce.
13. If you use a blender, puree the sauce in small batches and hold the lid with a towel while blending. Start with a low/slow speed.
14. Place the sauce in an airtight container. It will last one week in your fridge or up to 3 months in your freezer.

Macaroni Cheese Sauce

Nacho Cheese/Macaroni Cheese Sauce

- o Cheese: Great source of Vitamin B12, protein, fat and carries healthy bacteria. Cheese may even help your immune system from the natural bacteria and minerals found in dairy products. Like most fats and dairy, some people must be careful with how much cheese they consume. Otherwise, it may fluctuate unwanted weight or may cause discomfort in the stomach area.
    - **Yield:** 4 servings. ½ cup each.

Ingredients:

2 Tablespoons Stick Butter
2 Tablespoons All-Purpose flour
1 ½ cup 2% Milk
2 Tablespoons Sour Cream
2 Tablespoons Cream Cheese
1 ½ cup shredded Cheddar.
½ teaspoon Salt
¼ teaspoon Pepper
½ teaspoon Ground Mustard *(This secret ingredient gives cheese sauces that specific flavor profile.)*
Few Dashes of your favorite hot sauce

Nacho Cheese Sauce *(add in the flowing...)*
4oz can Diced Green Chilies, do not drain
4oz can Diced Tomatoes, drained.
1/8 teaspoon Cayenne Pepper

Directions:

1. Place a pot over medium to high heat. Add in butter and allow the butter to melt completely.
2. Slowly whisk in the flour to make a roux. Add the roux to turn a golden color. Do not walk away, though, or the roux might burn.
3. Slowly whisk in the milk. Add in about ½ cup at a time to ensure no clumps.
4. Next, whisk in the sour cream and cream cheese. Whisk out any clumps.
5. Whisk in the shredded cheese, salt, pepper, ground mustard, and hot sauce. Lightly simmer for 2 minutes. Enjoy.
6. If you are making nachos cheese sauce, you can add the chilis and tomatoes in step 5.

Snacks for All!

These snacks listed below are great options for all the chronic illnesses I list throughout my cookbook and people with "normal diets." All in moderation and verity, of course!

Snack List

Fresh Berries with Yogurt *(try and eat yogurt that has 10g of sugar or less per serving)*
- Veggies with Hummus or Ranch
- Low Sodium Popcorn
- Protein/Granola/Nut Bars *(minimal added sugars)*
- Dark Chocolate (small amount)
- 1 Hard-boiled Egg *(seasoned with pepper)*
- Cheese with Whole Grain Crackers and Sausage *(minimum amount and in moderation)*
- Fresh Fruit *(serving size= 1 whole fruit or 1 cup of cut fruit)*
- Trail Mix/Mixed Nuts *(serving size= ½ cup or ½ cup)*

Food that Helps Improve/Sustain Mental Health.

Brain Food: The brain and nervous system require many different nutrients (carbs, proteins, minerals) from food to continually build new proteins, cells, tissues, and effective body functioning. To obtain the most beneficial nutrients to improve and sustain your mental health, it is recommended to have a large variety of meals and snacks throughout the week. When eating, pay attention to how you feel after consuming the food. Does the food make you feel good and energized? Or does the food make you feel like you need to rest or take a nap? The better the food makes you feel, the better chance you can complete everyday tasks and sustain a healthy mental/physical state.

- **Complex Carbs:** These types of carbs will make you feel full for a more extended period than simple carbs.
  - Whole grains: brown rice, quinoa, millet, lentils, sweet potatoes, bulgur wheat, etc.
- **Lean Animal Proteins:** Provide your body and mind energy to react and think quickly.
  - Chicken, eggs, and whitefish.
- **Plant Proteins:** High in fiber and provide building blocks for muscle and tissues in your body. Plant proteins are low in calories, high in fiber, and contain other essential nutrients. Thus, they may also help with weight loss.
  - Nuts, edamame, lentils, quinoa, garbanzo beans, tofu, and tempeh.
- **Fatty Acids (omega 3):** Essential for proper brain and nervous system functions.
  - Nuts, fish, and flaxseeds.
- **Fruits and Vegetables:** Provide minerals the body and mind need to stay healthy, such as dietary fiber, vitamin C, A, potassium, and more.
  - Broccoli, spinach, kale, carrots, etc.
- **More Tips:**
  - Faith in the Lord: I always recommend praying to the Lord, reading his word, and putting all our worries in his hands. The Lord will bring us back and help us keep a healthy mental state!
  - Exercising regularly: 3-5 times a week for 30-40min.
  - Finding your support group!

Meal Ideas for Mental Health

Breakfast

- **Morning Refresher**
  (A warm, welcoming drink any time of the day! Ginger is excellent for digestion, while the beets and orange juice are packed with heart-healthy and immune-strengthening vitamins.)

Turmeric: Research has shown that turmeric can reduce inflammation, reduce arthritis flair-ups, help improve mental health, helps with PMS symptoms, is good for your skin, and has many more health benefits.

Turmeric: A golden spice that comes from India that is used in many cooking techniques and medicines. You may think ground turmeric is a little pricy in the store. But I am here to tell you it is worth the price. Turmeric can add such a bold and unique flavor to drinks, soups, curry, vegetables, and more, that you do not want to miss out on.

Ginger: Has a required taste. Once you learn how to utilize it, ginger can be a game-changer. There is something about ginger that gives dishes and beverages a refreshing taste. Lastly, it happens to be excellent for your digestive system.

TIP: You can buy fresh ginger in bulk, peel it all, and place it in a freezer bag. When you need ginger for a recipe, you can take a piece of ginger out of the freezer and use a sharp knife to shave the amount of ginger you need. Then put the rest of the ginger back in the freezer. The ginger will last for several months in the freezer, whereas it will only last a week or two in the fridge.

- **Yield**: 2 servings. 8oz each.

Ingredients:

1 large Cooked Beet (you can find pre-cooked beets in most grocery stores)
1 ½ cup Orange Juice.
¼ cup water
1 teaspoon Fresh Ginger, grated
½ teaspoon Ground Turmeric
¼ teaspoon liquid Stevia (optional)
Fresh Mint Leaves (garnish)

Directions:

1. Dice beets and place in a blender with the grated ginger, turmeric, and ¼ cup water, and blend until smooth.
2. Add in the orange juice, water, and stevia.
3. Pour into glasses, top with mint leaves, and enjoy.

Whole Wheat Biscuit Breakfast Sandwich Served with Fresh Fruit and a Side of Gravy

- **Whole Wheat Biscuit Breakfast Sandwich Served with Fresh Fruit**
  - Fruit and Whole Grains: Both ingredients are threaded with fiber. People who want to maintain a healthy diet/lifestyle are encouraged to learn that fiber is your friend and the backbone of nutrition. It helps with digestion, motor functions, maintaining a healthy weight, and simply feeling well. If you are not used to consuming a lot of fiber, your body might hate you because the fiber is being used to eliminate all the harmful toxins in your body. After a week or so, your body will adapt for the better.

    - **Yield:** 4 servings. Each serving = 1 sandwich and 1 cup of fruit.

Ingredients:

Biscuit Dough
¼ & 1/8 cup All-Purpose Flour
¾ cup Whole Wheat Flour
¼ teaspoon Salt
1, ¼ teaspoon Baking Powder
2 teaspoon Fresh Rosemary, minced

¼ cup or 2 oz Cold Butter, diced into cubes.
1/2 cup 2% milk

Sandwich filling

4 eggs
¼ cup Fresh Spinach Leaves, remove stems if desired.
4 slices of cheese *(your choice and type of cheese)*

Country Gravy Topping *(optional, ½ cup on top of each sandwich)*

1 ½ cups water
½ cup 2% milk
¾ cup country gravy packet mix

Fruit

1 cup Fresh Blueberries
1 cup Fresh Strawberries, sliced.

2 Bananas. Sliced into rounds.

Directions:

1. Preheat the oven to 425F.
2. In a bowl, whisk tother all the dry biscuit ingredients.
3. Next, use a pastry cutter, a fork, or your hands to mix the cold butter cubes into the flour. Keep mixing until you get marble-sized clumps of butter in the flour.
4. Use a wooden spoon to fold in the milk gently. The key is to barely mix the dough until it forms. If you over-mix, the biscuits will become dense after baking.
5. Lightly sprinkle flour onto a clean surface. You can use a rolling pin or your fingers to press the dough to about ½ inch thick. Use the rim of a glass or round cookie cutter (7 ¾ inches in diameter) to cut the biscuit dough into circles. Place the cut-out biscuits on a sprayed sheet pan or baking dish.
6. Bake for 12 minutes or until fully cooked through; set aside to cool.
7. Slice the berries and bananas and place them in a bowl. Set aside.
8. Place a pan over medium to high heat.
9. Spray the pan with cooking spray or 1 teaspoon of olive oil.
10. Place 4 eggs in the pan and season with salt and pepper to your likening.
11. Cook them for around 2 minutes on each side to achieve over medium. Place a slice of cheese on each egg.
12. Slice the biscuits in half with a serrated knife to create sandwich bread.
13. Place an egg with cheese on the base of each biscuit. Next, add on a ¼ cup of spinach and place the top of the biscuit on top.
14. Enjoy.
15. Gravy: Bring water to a boil in a small saucepan/pot. Whisk together the gravy mix and milk in a bowl. Once the water is boiling, slowly whisk in the mix/milk mixture to avoid clumps. Reduce to a simmer and allow to cook for 2 minutes or until you reach the desired thickness of the gravy. If the sauce becomes too thick, you can whisk in more water or milk. Pour over on top of snadwiches and dig in!

Lightly breaded Trout with Mixed Rice and Sautéed

Lunch

- **Lightly Dredged Trout Along with Mixed Rice and Sauteed Vegetables.**
  - ○ **Wild Rice:** This grain is rugged and earthy, which pairs nicely with white rice. Wild rice is high in dietary fiber. Fiber is one of the most significant nutrients your body needs for proper digestion. It keeps your cholesterol low and maintains a healthy weight. I love the umami flavor the grain can give a dish.
    - ▪ **Yield**: 4 Servings. Each Serving = 1/3 cup of rice, 1 fillet of trout, and ½ cup of veggies.

Ingredients:

Rice

½ cup Long Grain & Wild Rice Mix *(you can find a box of the two types of rice combined in the grocery store. Both are a cheaper and easier option.)*

1 cup Chicken Broth (see pages 16)

¼ cup Pine Nuts, toasted

¼ teaspoon Salt

1/8 teaspoon Pepper

Note: If the rice came with a seasoning packet, you could use that instead of salt and pepper.

Trout

4, 3oz Trout Fillets, skinless

½ cup All-Purpose Flour

½ teaspoon Salt

½ teaspoon Black Pepper

1/8 teaspoon Cayenne Pepper

½ teaspoon Dried Oregano

¼ teaspoon Garlic Powder

½ cup Vegetable Oil *(No oil needed if using an Air Fryer.)*

Veggies

1 Tablespoon Olive Oil

1 Small Head of Broccoli, cut florets and stems into bite-size pieces.

1 Yellow Squash, sliced into rounds.

1 Red Bell Pepper thinly sliced.

½ teaspoon Salt

½ teaspoon Pepper

2 Fresh Garlic Cloves, minced

Directions:

1. In a small pot, add both rice and chicken broth. Stir and bring to a boil. Once boiling, reduce to a simmer and cover the pot with a lid. Simmer for 20-30 minutes or until rice is tender. Stir occasionally.
2. In a bowl or on a curved plate, mix together flour, salt, pepper, cayenne, garlic powder, and oregano.
3. Place two large pans over medium to high heat. Add olive oil to one pan and vegetable oil to the other pan.
4. Add the veggies to the pan with olive oil. Stir veggies so they rest in a flat/even layer.
5. Meanwhile, place each trout fillet in the flour mixture. Evenly coat each fileted with a light layer of four.
6. Once the vegetable oil is hot, add in the trout. Try not to allow the trout fillets to touch each other.They need room to breathe/cook evenly.
   a. TIP: If you have an air fryer, you can also get the same results without the oil! Put your air fryer on the fish setting or at 325F for 15 minutes. Drizzle or spray the fish with olive oil before placing it in the air fryer to achieve a golden and crispy layer.
7. Stir the veggies and add garlic, salt, and pepper.
8. Once the fish is golden color, flip over to allow the other side to be golden. (If you are using an air fryer, flip over the trout halfway through cooking as well)
9. I like my broccoli to have a little texture, so that is why I did not precook the broccoli separately. Once the veggies are tender, remove from the heat.'
10. When the internal temperature of the fish reaches 145F, it is ready!
11. Plate and enjoy!

Lightly Fried Tempeh Along with Rice and Saluted Vegetables.

Or

- **Lightly Fried Tempeh Along with Rice and Salted Vegetables.**

  o **Tempeh:** Fermented soy product that may be considered tofu's cousin. A superfood that has many positive benefits for your body. Tempeh is a complete plant protein that contains prebiotics. Prebiotics helps improve your bone health and immune systems.

    ▪ **Yield:** 4 Servings. Each serving = 1/3 cup rice, 3 oz tempeh, and ½ cup veggies.

Ingredients:

12oz package of tempeh
Vegetable oil

Rice: As seen above
Veggies: As seen above

Directions:

1. Place a thin layer of oil in a shallow pan.
2. Heat pan over medium to high heat
3. Cut tempeh into bite-size cubes.
4. When oil is hot, add tempeh cubes, brown, and get crispy on each side of the cubes. When the tempeh is evenly crisp, remove it from the pan and sprinkle it with salt.
5. See the above recipes on pages 29-30 for rice and veg.
6. Enjoy!

Sweet Potato Black Bean Chili

Dinner

- **Sweet Potato Black Bean Chili**

  (_the first time I had this was in culinary School. This recipe_ is _impeccable. Trust me, you will not even miss the meat in a traditional chili!_)

  o Sweet Potatoes: I have a big, sweet tooth. So, anything with a natural healthy sweetness is one of my go-to items! Some people may be surprised that sweet potatoes are good for you because of their name and being in the potato family. They are particularly good for gut functions. Sweet potatoes contain insoluble and soul-able fiber. The body cannot digest those types of fiber, so the digestive tract traps fiber and uses it to provide health to the gut.

    - **Yield**: 4 servings. About 12oz bowls each.

Ingredients:

1lb or 1 large Sweet Potato, peeled and cut into bite sizer cubes.
1 teaspoon Smoked Paprika.
1 1/2 teaspoon salt
2 T olive oil
1 diced onion
2 garlic cloves, minced
1 small Jalapeno, minced.
1 Tablespoon Chili powder
1/2 Tablespoon ground cumin
½ teaspoon dried oregano
1, 4oz can Roasted Green Chiles
1, 15 oz can dice tomatoes (save juice)

3 cups vegetable broth
½ teaspoon Granulated Sugar
2 teaspoons Unsweetened Cocoa Powder
1, 15 oz can Black Beans, drained and rinsed
Pinch of Cayenne Pepper
Corn Starch Slurry (1T cornstarch, 2t water)

Toppings _(Optional)_
Shredded Cheese
Sour Cream
Chopped Cilantro

Directions:

1. Preheat the oven to 450 F and line a sheet pan with parchment paper.
2. Toss sweet potato cubes in a bowl with oil to coat the potatoes, ½ teaspoon of salt, and the paprika—spread potatoes in a single layer on the prepared sheet pan.
3. Bake in the oven for 20 minutes or until they are almost tender. Remove from oven and allow to cool.
4. Heat a large pot over medium to high heat, and add 1T of olive oil, diced onion, garlic, jalapeno, chili powder, cumin, and dried oregano. Cook and stir for 5 minutes or until the onions are translucent.
5. Add in the canned tomatoes, canned chilies, both of their juices and 2 cups of vegetable stock. Stir, and bring to a simmer. Next, add ¼ teaspoon salt, sugar, and cocoa powder. Simmer for 30 minutes.
6. Stir in the rinsed black beans, cooked sweet potatoes, and a pinch of cayenne. Suppose the chili appears too thick; add in 1 more cup of vegetable broth. Cover the pot, and simmer for another 15-20 min. Adjust seasoning if need be.
7. If the chili is too thin, bring it to a bowl and stir in the cornstarch slurry. Reduce heat and allow to thicken for a few minutes.
8. Add your topping of sour cream, cheese, and cilantro, and enjoy.

Spaghetti Squash Hash with Kielbasa Sausage

- **Spaghetti Squash Hash with Kielbasa Sausage**
  - o Spaghetti Squash: A low-calorie and carb option is an excellent substitute for pasta or other heavy-carb items. Spaghetti squash contains fiber, vitamin C, vitamin B6, and manganese. Manganese helps the body form connective tissue. It may also help with hormone regulation and bone health.

    - **Yield**: 4 Servings.

Ingredients:

1 Spaghetti Squash
1 kielbasa sausage, sliced on the bias.
1 Yellow Onion thinly sliced.
4oz Fresh Mushrooms, sliced
chopped.
2 Cups Fresh Spinach
1 small Green Bell Pepper, diced
2 large Fresh Garlic Cloves, minced
1 teaspoon Garam marsala
4 eggs
¼ cup Grated Parmesan.
Salt and Pepper to taste.
Olive Oil
Black Finishing Salt, garnish (optional)

Garam Masala
1 Tablespoon Ground Cumin
1 teaspoon Ground Coriander
½ teaspoon Ground Black Pepper
1 teaspoon Ground Cinnamon
½ teaspoon Ground Cloves
½ teaspoon Ground Nutmeg
1 teaspoon Ground Cardamom
½ teaspoon Salt

Directions:

1. Preheat oven to 400F.
2. Cut spaghetti squash within half lengthwise. Remove the seeds.

3. Drizzle the squash with olive oil and sprinkle with salt and pepper.
4. Place the squash quarters in a baking dish and cut side down.
5. Add ½ cup of water to the baking dish, cover with foil, and bake for 30-45 minutes. Remove and allow to cool.
    a. TIP: In a rush? Skip the oven and go straight to the microwave!
        i. Complete steps 2 and 3 above.
        ii. Place squash in a microwave-safe dish or bowl.
        iii. Add water into the bowl and cover with a lid or plastic wrap. Microwave for 3-5 minutes or until the squash is tender. Remove and allow to cool.
6. In the meantime, heat a large pan over medium heat. Spray the pan with cooking spray and allow the pan to heat up.
7. Add the sausage and allow the sausage pieces to brown on both sides. Remove and set aside.
8. add 1-2 Tablespoons of olive oil to the pan.
9. Add onion, bell pepper, and mushroom. Stir into a single layer and sauté for 5 minutes.
10. Next, stir in the garlic and spinach. Sauté for 3 more minutes. Now add the garam masala, salt, and pepper and stir to coat evenly. Reduce to low heat.
11. Meanwhile, heat an additional pan over medium heat. Spray with cooking spray and crack 4 eggs into the pan. Cook eggs for 2-3 minutes for sunny-side-up eggs.
12. Shred the squash out of its skin.
13. Add the shredded spaghetti squash and parmesan to the pan with the veggies stir.
14. Top sausage and eggs. Enjoy.

Chronic Obstructive Pulmonary Disease (COPD)

COPD is a long-term disease that affects the lungs and the respiratory system making it hard to breathe and maintain energy. COPD may be caused by infection, smoking tobacco, breathing in secondhand smoke, or all other forms of air pollution.

- **Foods That Help Maintain COPD**
  - Eat 20 to 30 grams of fiber each day from items such as bread, whole grains, pasta, nuts, seeds, fruits, and vegetables. The fiber helps regulate bowel movements. However, avoid heavy amounts of food items that may make the person have gas. Gas can cause bloating and result in hard breathing.
  - Eat a good source of protein at least twice a day to help maintain strong respiratory muscles.
    - Good choices include low amounts of eggs, lean meats/fish, nuts, and legumes.
  - Potassium is vital to lung function,
    - To consume potassium, eat Apple stone fruits such as apricots and peaches.
  - Fresh vegetables, fresh fruits, and herbs have great antioxidants/vitamins for body and lung support.
    - Blueberries, red cabbage, pumpkin, beets.
  - Consume plenty of non-carbonated beverages to help keep mucus levels down. Carbonated beverages can cause bloating = harder to breathe.

High Protein Banana Oat Pancakes with a Blueberry Syrup

Menu Ideas for COPD

Breakfast

- **High Protein Banana Oat Pancakes with a Blueberry Syrup**
  - Oats: A fiber and vitamin-enriched whole gain. Like most whole grains, oats can make you feel fuller and stay full for a more extended amount of time than processed carbs. Oats can help you lose or maintain your body weight from the high amounts of soluble fiber and vitamins. This whole grain can produce nitric oxide in the body from its antioxidants. Nitric oxide may help dilate blood vessels, resulting in better blood flow in the body. Thus, oats can also help control blood sugar levels and cholesterol.
  - **Blueberries:** A great snack or topping to have any time. They are rich in antioxidants and do wonders for the body and mind. Some may even say blueberries are the king of antioxidants that your body will suck right up! Blueberries have many powers, such as heart health, improving brain and memory functions, may help with UTIs, may reduce muscle damage from excise, and more!
    - **Yield**: 4 servings. Each serving = 1 pancake and 2 Tablespoons of syrup. You can serve it with eggs if desired. These pancakes also go nicely with Morning Refresher on page

Ingredients:

Pancakes
2 Whole Bananas
2 Eggs
1 cup Whole Oats
¼ cup Rice Flour
1 teaspoon Vanilla Extract
1 teaspoon Baking Powder
1 scoop (30grams/1 serving size on the container) of your favorite Protein Powder (I recommend vanilla or chocolate flavor)

Spices
1 teaspoon Cinnamon
¼ teaspoon Cardamon
¼ teaspoon Nutmeg
¼ teaspoon salt

Syrup
8oz Fresh Blueberries
½ cup Water
¼ cup Granulated Sugar.
½ teaspoon Vanilla Extract
½ Lemon (Fresh Lemon Zest and Juice)
   Corn Starch Slurry, *last step* (1 Tablespoon corn starch, around 2 teaspoons) should be a simi thin mixture, with some resistance when stirring.

Garnish
Powdered Sugar

Directions:

1. Put whole oats into a blender, food processor, or spice grinder until the oats become a powder.
2. In a large bowl, mash the bananas with a fork until smooth.
3. Stir in the eggs and vanilla!
4. Fold in the oats, rice flour, and baking powder. Then fold in the spices. Set aside.
5. Add all the syrup ingredients; expect the slurry.
6. Stir all the ingredients until sugar dissolves and other components are incorporated. Allow the mixture to simmer for 10 minutes.
7. Meanwhile, place a large pan over medium heat spray with cooking spray.
8. Use a ½ cup measuring cup to pour the batter into the heated pan. Spray the pan each time before placing more batter in the pan.
9. Allow each side to become golden brown and remove it from the pan.
10. Once the syrup has been simmering for 5 minutes, give it a nice stir to smash some of the blueberries.
11. Make the slurry by mixing the cornstarch and water in a small bowl. While whisking the syrup, slowly pour in the slurry. Allow the syrup to come to a gentle boil and cook until you reach your desired thickness.
12. Serve syrup over pancakes.

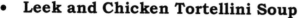

Lunch

• **Leek and Chicken Tortellini Soup**

○ **Leeks:** A part of the onion family. They contain vitamin A carotenoids. These carotenoids work in the body while helping with vision, immune function, and cell communications. Leeks also have vitamin K, which helps with blood clouting for the body and heart health.

▪ When it comes to soup, sometimes I prefer leeks over onions. Leeks give a unique texture and flavor to your favorite soup/dish.

▪ **Yield**: 4 Servings

Ingredients:

2 Tablespoons Stick Butter
12oz Skinless Chicken Breast, trim off any fat, and medium dice.
1 teaspoon Smoked Paprika.
¼ cup White Onion, small diced
¼ cup Carrots, small diced
¼ cup Celery, small diced
½ cup Mushrooms, chopped.
1 Leek, sliced into thin rounds. Discard dark green part/ends
¼ teaspoon Ground Turmeric
½ teaspoon Black Pepper
1 teaspoon salt
1 teaspoon Dried Thyme
32oz Chicken Broth (see pages 16)
1lb Tri-Colored Cheese Tortellini
½ cup canned White Beans, drained and rinsed.

Directions:

1. Pat chicken completely dry.
2. In a large pot, melt 1 Tablespoon of butter over medium to high heat.
3. Add in the diced chicken and paprika. Stir and allow the chicken to thoroughly cook. TIP: If the chicken is releasing water into the pot, remove all water for the chicken to brown.
4. Remove the cooked chicken and set it aside.
5. Remove any water that is left in the pan.
6. Add the remaining 1 Tablespoon of butter and all the prepared veggies.
7. Add in all the remaining spices and give a good stir. All veggies to soften for 3-5 minutes.
8. Once the veggies are cooked, stir in 1 Tablespoon of flour. Allow cooking for one more minute.
9. Deglaze the pan (scrape up all the cooked-on bits on the bottom of the pan) while whisking in the vegetable broth. Bring to a boil, then add the tortellini and beans.
10. Reduce to a simmer and add back in the chicken. Allow to cook for 3 minutes or until the tortellini is cooked to your liking.
11. Enjoy!

Tofu Grain and Veggie Bowl

Dinner

- **Tofu Grain and Veggie Bowl (Asian Inspired)**
  - **Quinoa:** A wonderful whole-grain option if you are trying to increase your protein intake. In my opinion, it is beneficial for individuals to consume both plant and animal proteins to obtain a well-rounded diet. Quinoa is an edible cereal/seed grain that contains antioxidants called flavonoids. As the flavonoids enter the body stream, they may create anti-inflammatory, anti-viral, anti-cancer, and anti-depressant effects. Lastly, quinoa is gluten-free and high in fiber.
  - **Cabbage:** One of those unappreciated vegetables. Not only is cabbage cheap, but it is also very nutritious. I like my cabbage raw in slaws and cooked with many flavors. This vegetable is excellent for your bones because of the calcium, magnesium, and potassium found in cabbage. Cabbage also may reduce headaches and may help with skincare.
    - **Yield:** 4 servings. Each Serving = 3-4oz tofu, ¼ cup cabbage, ¼ cup carrots, 2/3 cup quinoa/rice mixture, ¼ cup arugula, 1 Tablespoon sauce, 1 teaspoon chopped peanuts, ¼ teaspoon sesame seeds, and red pepper flakes.

Ingredients:

Tofu Marinade *(chill overnight)*
12-16oz Firm Tofu, diced into ½-inch cubes.
¼ cup water
4 Tablespoons Soy Sauce, low sodium
2 Tablespoons Sweet Chili Sauce
1 large garlic clove, minced.
2 green onions, diced.
1 teaspoon Fresh Ginger, grated

<u>Slaw</u> *(prepare and chill overnight)*
1 cup Raw Purple Cabbage, shredded.
1 teaspoon Apple Cider Vinegar
1 teaspoon Olive oil
1/8 teaspoon salt
1/8 teaspoon Pepper
¼ teaspoon Granulated Sugar

<u>Other Ingredients</u>

¾ cup Raw Tri-Colored Quinoa
2 cups Vegetable Broth (see pages13-15)
¾ cup Raw White Rice
1 Tablespoon Olive Oil
2 cups Shredded Carrots
1 teaspoon Olive Oil
1/8 teaspoon salt
1/8 teaspoon pepper
1 cup Raw Arugula

<u>Peanut Sauce</u>
2/3 cup Peanut Butter
¼ teaspoon Ground Ginger
1 Tablespoon Honey
2 Tablespoons Soy Sauce
½ teaspoon Fish Sauce
1 teaspoon Tahini
1 teaspoon Sweet Chili Sauce
½ cup Water, *or more depending on how thin you want the sauce to be.*

<u>Garnish</u>
1 teaspoon Black Sesame Seeds
1 teaspoon Red Pepper Flakes
4 teaspoons Roasted Peanuts

Directions:

Day Before

1. In a container, mix all ingredients for the tofu marinade. Then add in the diced tofu. Make sure the tofu is wholly covered with the liquid. Cover with lid and place in the fridge overnight

2. In a container, mix all the ingredients for the slaw marinade. Then add in the shredded cabbage and stir to coat the cabbage evenly. Cover with a lid and place in the fridge overnight.

Next-Day!

3. Place the raw quinoa and 1 cup vegetable broth in a small pot. Stir and then bring to a boil. Once boiling, stir again, reduce to a simmer, and cover the pot with a lid. Allow to cook for 20 minutes or until the quinoa is done. Hint: the quinoa is done when you see rings form around the quinoa seeds.

4. Cook the rice the same way in a separate pot with 2 cups of vegetable broth.

5. When the rice and quinoa are both cooked, mix

6. Whisk together all the ingredients for the peanut sauce in a small saucepan over medium to high heat.

7. When peanut butter has melted and combined ingredients, turn the burner on low and stir occasionally.

8. Place a small sauté pan over medium heat. Add 1 teaspoon olive oil, salt, pepper, and shredded carrots. Sautee until the carrots are soft and stir occasionally.

9. Place a large pan over medium to high heat. Add in 1 Tablespoon of Olive Oil and allow the pan to get hot.

10. Remove the tofu from the marinade and add the marinated tofu to the pan in a single layer. Allow the tofu to cook on all sides.

11. Remove the slaw from the fridge.

12. Place all the prepared and raw items next to each other in a bowl, as seen in the picture. Sprinkle the garnishes on top of each bowl or as desired.

13. I hope you enjoy this flavorful and nutritious dish!

Mocktail

- **Blood Orange and Lime Mocktail**

○ **Blood Orange:** Like navel oranges, blood oranges are also a great source of Vitamin C. However, blood oranges typically contain more vitamin A and fiber than navel organs. When Vitamin A enters your system, it helps vital organs in the body function properly, such as your kidneys, heart, and lungs. Blood oranges also have a delightful taste and color!

- **Yield**: 4 Servings. 8oz each.

Ingredients:

16oz Blood Orange Juice
4oz Coconut water
2oz Fresh Lime juice
4oz Water
1 Teaspoon Liquid Stevia
Ice for each glass

Garnish
Fresh Mint

Directions:

1. Mix all ingredients in a large pitcher.
2. Pour the mixed drink over ice into each glass. Place one slice of orange on the rim of a glass, and a three-leave cluster of mint leaves in the drink
3. Enjoy!

Maintain Diabetes

Diabetes is a disease that causes blood sugar or blood glucose to spike to extremely high levels when eating certain foods. The hormone insulin is what transfers glucose into the cells to produce energy for the body.

Menu Ideas for Diabetes!

Breakfast

- **Plain Oatmeal** topped with sliced nuts and fresh fruit.
- **Toasted Whole Wheat Bagel** topped with 2 Tablespoons of peanut butter, avocado, or cream cheese.

- **Egg Bites**

(you can make these ahead of time! They last five days in the fridge or three months in the freezer. Reheat in the microwave for 30-60 seconds.)

○ **Arugula:** Filled with folate, Calcium, Potassium, and vitamins B, C, and K. This leafy green can help with blood clotting and healthy heart/nerve functions. Arugula has a unique flavor that complements many flavors and goes specifically well with eggs! s

- **Yield**: 10-12 egg bites, 2-3 per serving.

Ingredients:

9 large eggs
¼ cup shredded Pepper Jack Cheese
¼ cup shredded Parmesan
½ teaspoon Ground Cumin
¼ teaspoon Dried Italian Herbs
½ teaspoon Sea Salt
¼ teaspoon Freshly Ground White Pepper. *(If you want to achieve a bold flavor*

from the white pepper, lightly toast the peppercorns and then grind them for
the best flavor results.)
1 teaspoon Minced Garlic
½ cup diced seeded Red Bell Pepper or Roasted Red Peppers.

Garnish
Fresh Arugula

Directions:

1. Preheat the oven to 400°F. Grease/spray a 12-cup average-sized muffin pan.
2. Combine the eggs, cheese, cumin, sea salt, and white pepper in a bowl and
   whisk until everything is combined and the eggs obtain some air in them.
3. Sauté the bell peppers and kale in a pan with 1T of olive oil over medium heat
   for 5 minutes or until tender. Add in the garlic and sauté for one more minute.
   (If the pepper is already roasted/cooked, skip this step and mix the garlic in a
   bowl with the bell peppers.)
4. Evenly distribute the diced bell peppers among the muffin tins. Pour the egg
   mixture over the veggies, filling each cup about three-fourths full. The egg
   will rise, so you do not want to fill them all the way.
5. Bake for 16-18 minutes or until the eggs are set and cooked through.
   You can use a toothpick to test. If the eggs are done, place the toothpick in
   the center of the egg. If the pick comes out clean, the eggs are done. Allow
   eggs to cool slightly in the pan before taking them out.
6. Make sure to fully cool the egg bites before placing them into a
   fridge/freezer container for food safety purposes.

Lunch

- **Turkey Sandwich With Multigrain Tortilla Chips**
  (deli meat is not always recommended for people with diabetes. Because it is incredibly high in sodium and additives, which can affect your insulin. However, if you love sandwiches, you can eat them once or twice a week if your other meals those days are low in sodium.)

  o   Avocados: One of the healthiest fats you can eat. They contain heart-healthy monounsaturated fatty acids. Like most fruits, avocados are also filled with fiber and other healthy-function nutrients. Lastly, a _fun little tip_, avocados contain vitamin E. eating foods with Vitamin E may help reduce hot flashes if you experience those.
  - **Yield**: 1 Serving.

Ingredients:

2 T Avocado, Mashed
4 Thin Slices of Cucumbers
2 T Roasted Red Pepper, Diced or Sliced.
¼ cup Spinach, Mixed Greens, or Arugula
2 Slices of Seeded Rye Bread (See Pages 68-70)
       Or two slices of your favorite whole-wheat bread
3oz of low-sodium deli turkey meat
 1 Cup of Multigrain Tortilla Chips, _you can find multigrain seeded tortilla chips in most grocery stores._

Directions:

1. Spread avocado on one side of the bread.
2. Lay around 4 slices of turkey on top of the avocado.
3. Next, add the cucumbers, roasted red peppers, and mixed greens.
4. Top with another slice of bread and serve with chips.

Salmon Salad

- **Salmon Salad**

  (great to make the night before or on your meal prep day!)
    - ○ Salmon: A rich and fatty fish, where a little can go a long way. Salmon contains omega-3 fatty acids, vitamin B's, selenium, and more. Selenium is a mineral found in soil and certain foods like salmon. Studies have shown that consuming a small amount of selenium may help protect bone health, decrease thyroid antibodies for people with thyroid disease, and may even reduce the risk of cancer.

        - **Yield:** 4 servings, each serving = 3-4oz salmon fillet, 2 Tablespoons corn, 1 Mushroom, 1 Tablespoon sunflower seeds, 2 Tablespoons cucumber, 1-2 cups of salad mix, 1 hardboiled egg, ¼ cup green beans, and 2 Tablespoons dressing.

Ingredients:

12-16oz skinless salmon fillet (salmon is high in omega 3, fatty acids. Fatty acids are an essential nutrient your body needs to function correctly.)

    -If you do not want to try the salmon, you can easily switch it out with any other fish, plant protein, and poultry.

1-2 Corn on The Cob

4 large Fresh Button Mushrooms

4 Tablespoons of Sunflower seeds

1 Cucumber, diced *(I like to peel strips around the cucumber and leave the seeds in)*

4 Hard-Boiled Eggs, sliced.

4-8 cups Salad Mix (Mixed Greens, Spinach, and Arugula).

8 Tablespoons Balsamic Vinaigrette, Honey Mustard, or Dressing of Choice

<u>6oz Fresh Green Beans</u>

2 Tablespoon Olive Oil

½ teaspoon Cumin

¼ teaspoon Salt

¼ teaspoon pepper

Directions:

1. Preheat oven to 350F.

Eggs

2. Place the eggs in a pot and cover the eggs with water. Bring the water to a gentle boil and set a timer for 10 minutes.
3. Once the 10 minutes are up, remove eggs from the pot and place them in ice water place in the fridge. Allow eggs to cool completely before peeling.
4. Run eggs under cold water as you are peeling them.
5. Slice eggs.

Green Beans

6. Trim off the ends of the green beans and cut them in half.
7. Place a small pot over high heat. Fill the pot with water and bring to a boil.
8. Once the water is boiling, add the green beans and blanch for 2 minutes or until the beans are bright green. Remove green beans and place them in ice water; this will shock them. Once the beans are cooled, remove them from the ice bath.
9. Place a pan over medium heat. Add in 1 Tablespoon of olive oil. Allow the pan to heat up, and then add in the green beans. Season with salt, pepper, and cumin, and sauté for 3-5 minutes or until tender. (I like to leave a little crunch/texture.)

Corn

10. Cut the Corn off the cob and place it on a sheet pan. Drizzle the corn kernels with olive oil and with ¼ teaspoon of salt and pepper.
11. Toss/stir corn kernels around and bake in the oven for 5-10 minutes. Remove from oven/sheet pan and allow to cool.

Salmon

12. Season both sides of the salmon fillet with salt and pepper to taste. You can also season the fish with dried Italian herbs.
13. Place a pan over medium to high heat and drizzle the pan with olive oil. Place salmon in a pan with ¼ cup of water and cover with a lid. Steam the salmon until it reaches 145F.
    a. TIP: I have found that steaming salmon takes away some of the fishy and rich flavors that some people may not like.
14. Place your greens on a plate, container, or bowl with the leafy greens. Top the greens with sliced avocado, sunflower seeds, sliced boiled egg, corn, salmon, green beans, cucumber, and dressing.
    o I also love buying premade **salad kits** at the store! They are always a great option as well for lunch, dinner, or a side dish.

Spiced-Rubbed Pork Loin Accompanied by An Ancient Grain Salad

Dinner

- **Spiced-Rubbed Pork Loin Accompanied by An Ancient Grain Salad**
  - ○ **Bulgur Wheat:** Also known as an ancient grain. Bulgur wheat is enriched with many vitamins and minerals that can reduce chronic disease risks within the body.
  - ○ **Edamame:** A type of soy by-product. Enriched with protein, vitamin K, antioxidants, and fiber. Vitamin K is essential for blood flow, blood clotting, and bone metabolism.
    - ▪ **Yield:** 4 servings, each serving = 4oz pork, 2oz sauce, ½ cup salad

Ingredients:

Bulgur Wheat and Edamame Salad
¼ cup Red Onions, diced.
Fresh Lemon Zest from 1 lemon
Fresh Lemon Juice from 1 lemon
1 teaspoon Balsamic Vinegar
2 teaspoons Olive Oil
¼ teaspoon Salt and Pepper
½ cup Raw Bulgur Wheat
1 cup Water
3 Tablespoons Fresh Cilantro, chopped.
3 Tablespoons Fresh Mint, chopped.
3 Tablespoons Fresh Parsley, chopped.
1 ½ cups Edamame, thawed, shelled, and fully cooked.

Garnish *(optional)*
2 Tablespoons Feta Cheese
1 Tablespoon Pine Nuts, toasted.

Pork Tenderloin
16oz Raw Pork Tenderloin
1 Tablespoon Garam Masala (See Page 37)

Mushroom Sauce
8 oz Mushrooms, sliced.
1 Tablespoon Stick Butter

1 Tablespoon Flour
2 Garlic Cloves, minced.
½ cup Vegetable Broth (see pages 13-15)
1 cup half & half
1 cup Shredded Parmesan
2 teaspoons Fresh Thyme
¼ teaspoon Salt
¼ teaspoon Black Pepper

Directions:

1. Preheat the oven to 425 degrees F.

Bulgur Wheat and Edamame Beans Salad

2. In a bowl, combine red onions, lemon juice, zest, balsamic vinegar, olive oil, salt, and pepper. Whisk together. Cover and place in refrigerator.
3. Bring water to a boil in a small pot. Stir in bulgur. Remove from heat and cover for 15 minutes or until tender and all liquid is absorbed.
4. Remove the bulgur wheat from the pot and allow it to cool.

Pork Tenderloin

5. In the meantime: put ½ cup of water in a baking casserole dish. Coat tenderloin with olive oil. Season the whole loin with the garam masala and place it in the baking dish. Place in the oven for 30-45 minutes or until the pork reaches 145 degrees F. Let rest for 10 minutes before slicing the pork into 1/4-inch-thick round slices.

Mushroom Sauce

6. Place a pan over medium-high heat and add butter and mushrooms. Sautee until mushrooms have absorbed the butter and are tender.
7. Next, add the garlic and whisk in flour. Sauté for 1 minute.
8. Slowly whisk in veg broth and half & half. Bring to a gentle boil and then reduce to a light simmer. Next, whisk in parmesan and fresh thyme—season with salt and pepper to taste.
9. The sauce should lightly coat the back of the spoon for thickness desirability.

Salad Continued

10. Grab the marinade from the refrigerator and in the bulgur wheat   and the rest of the ingredients. Stir and enjoy. Top with garnish.

Brownie Mix/Ingredients

Fudgy Black Bean Brownies

<u>*Dessert* </u>*(in moderation)*

- **Fudgy Black Bean Brownies**
  (I had black bean brownies for the first time in my nutrition labs! They are super tasty, and you can barely tell they are flourless bean brownies.) My secret ingredients are beets. This recipe is a great way to sneak superfoods into your family's diet. I am sure your kids, family, and friends will love them.
  - o Beets: Packed with essential nutrients like nitric oxide, folate, and fiber. They help maintain your blood pressure while possibly reducing the risks of future heart problems. Beets also help improve athletic performance (stamina), help with digestion, and may help your body fight inflammation.
    - **Yield:** 8-12 servings.

Ingredients:

1 1/4 cups Dark Chocolate Chunks

1 15.5 oz can Black Beans, rinsed and drained.

1/4 cup Cocoa Powder, unsweetened

2 eggs

1/3 cup Olive Oil.

1/4 teaspoon Cinnamon

2 teaspoons Vanilla Extract

1/4 teaspoon salt

1/2 teaspoon Baking Powder

1 tablespoon Instant Coffee

1   teaspoon Powdered Stevia

1 teaspoon Organic Cane Sugar

1 cup of Purred Beets. *(You can buy precooked or canned beets at most grocery stores.). Or roast fresh beets in your oven at 400F for about 40min or until fork tender. Remove/discard outer skin.*

Directions:

1. Preheat oven to 350F.
2. Spay an 8 x 8 baking dish or a 10 x 10 pie plate with cooking spray. Line with parchment paper and spray the parchment paper with cooking spray.
3. Place beets in a blender with ¼ cup of water and blend until smooth. Add more water if the puree is too thick or you are not able to get a smooth consistency.

4. Place beans and half of the olive oil into a blender or food processor and blend until completely smooth. *(If you do not have a food processor, you can mash the beans as smooth as possible (or use an electric mixer).*

5. Next, add the pureed beans and the rest of the olive oil, and beat into a bowl. Add in all the other ingredients and mix with a wooden spoon. (The key is not to over mix. As you stir the batter, just barely bring all the ingredients together so everything is evenly distributed.

6. Use a rubber spatula to scrape the sides of the bowl and pour the batter into the prepared baking dish.

7. Bake for 30- 40 minutes or until cooked through. <u>TIP:</u> Stick a toothpick or butter knife in the center of the brownies. If the toothpick comes out clean, they are done.

8. Allow to cool, and then serve!

Cocktails

- **Minty Mojito**
  ○ **Mint Leaves:** Brings a very refreshing flavor to any drink and some dishes. Mint may help reduce body pains, cold symptoms, and indigestion.

    ▪ **Yield:** 2 Servings. 12oz glass each.

Ingredients:

10 Fresh Mint Leaves
2 – 4 drops of Liquid Stevia (to taste)
1-2 Fresh Limes
3 ounces white rum
8oz Club Soda
8oz Coconut Water _(I used naturally pink coconut water)_

Garnish
Fresh Mint Leaves
Lime wedges/slices

Directions:

1. Muddle/smash the mint leaves with your fingers to release the natural oils/aromatics.
2. Add 5 mint leaves, 1-2 drops of stevia, juice from ½ a lime, and 1 ½ oz of rum to each cocktail shaker or glass. Shake or stir until desired.
3. Pour each drink mix into a glass filled ¼ way up with ice. Top off with 4oz soda water and 4oz coconut water each.
4. Garnish with mint sprigs and lime wedges.
5. Enjoy!

Acceptable Alcholic Beverages

- **Dry Red and White Wines**
  - ○ Dry wines have a low sugar content and are the best option when managing diabetes. Sweet wines and dessert wines will likely raise blood sugar levels.
- **Lite or Low-Carb Beer**
  - ○ Beers that are low in carbs and sugars are another great option! Look for lite beers with 5g of carbs or fewer per 12oz serving.
- **Hard Seltzer**
  - ○ Most hard seltzers are gluten-free or have minimal carbs, no sugar, and very few calories.
- **Bloody Mary's**
  - ○ This classic mixed drink with low-sodium tomato juice, black pepper, and celery sticks is a fun way to keep your blood sugar stable.

Alzheimer's Disease

Alzheimer's is a very deviating disease not only for the individual with the disease. But especially for their loved ones and caregivers. Alzheimer's is a disease that destroys brain cells. As the disease progresses, more and more memory/motor functions will be lost. One of those diseases is continually being researched to discover new possibilities of cause and cure. Sadly, there is currently no cure for Alzheimer's. However, there may be some strategies and lifestyle behaviors people can do to possibly prevent having the disease.

Positive Lifestyle choices

- Regular Physical Exercise
  - Exercising positively impacts your brain cells by increasing blood and oxygen flow in the brain. Resulting in healthy memory and motor functions.
- How and What You Eat
  - "Current evidence suggests that heart-healthy eating may also help protect the brain. Heart-healthy eating includes limiting the intake of sugar and saturated fats and making sure to eat plenty of fruits, vegetables, and whole grains. No one diet is best. Two diets that have been studied and may be beneficial to lowering the risk of Alzheimer's are the DASH (Dietary Approaches to Stop Hypertension) diet and the Mediterranean diet." (Alzheimer's Association, 2021).
  - The DASH diet includes mainly vegetables, fat-free dairy, whole grains, fish, beans, and more.
  - Mediterranean Diet: primarily fish, whole grains, and veggies
  - The key is to limit sugar, processed foods, and high amounts of sodium.
- Continually Learning to Keep Your Brain Active.
  - Keeping your brain active with new topics and activities is one strategy to keep your memory young.
- Keeping Regular Social Group and Participating in Activities
  - When we plan meetings, gatherings, and activities with our friends and family makes us have a schedule. Having a regular and irregular schedule can keep our brains active.
- Being Safe
  - Take all safety protection seriously.
    - Always wear your seat belts and wear helmets
    - Avoid putting any tripping hazards in your home/yard.
  - There may be evidence that links head trauma to developing Alzheimer's.

Alzheimer Menu Ideas

Breakfast

- **Muesli**

○ Some people may also call muesli overnight oats.

○ Great for breakfast on the go!

○ **Hemp Seeds:** Rich in omega 6 and 3 fatty acids and are rich in protein. Hemp seeds have been used for heart health and may reduce the risks of heart disease. They also may reduce PMS and menopause symptoms.

▪ **Yield:** 4 servings. ½ cup each.

Ingredients:

1 cup Whole Oats

¼ cup Dried Apricots, chopped.

¼ cup Mixed Nuts, chopped.

1 Tablespoon Chia Seeds

1 Tablespoon Hemp seeds

1 teaspoon Ground Flax Seeds *(If you do not ground the flax seeds, you will not gain any nutritional value. If you swallow a whole seed, they are likely to not digest in your system.)*

1 Tablespoon Sunflower Seeds or Pumpkin Seeds

½ teaspoon Ground Cinnamon

Pinch of Salt

1 Tablespoon Brown Sugar

1 teaspoon Vanilla Extract

¼ cup Yogurt *(10g sugar or less per serving on the yogurt container)*

1 ¼ cup Almond Milk or Soy Milk, unsweetened

Directions:

1. Preheat the oven to 350F.
2. Place nuts, oats, and seeds on a sheet pan in a single layer.
3. Bake in the oven for 5 minutes or until lightly toasted. _TIP:_ toasting will give the muesli a bolder flavor for your taste buds to enjoy.
4. Remove from oven and all toasted items to completely cool.
    a. Or use a dry pan and toast the seeds/nuts/oats on the stove.
5. Combine the toasted items with dried apricots, vanilla, cinnamon, salt, brown sugar, yogurt, and milk. Stir to combine.
6. Place in an airtight container and place in the fridge; the oats, nuts, and seeds will absorb the liquid and make a lovely thick Muesli for breakfast.
7. If the muesli turns out to be too thick for your liking, stir in ¼ cup of milk at a time until the preferred thickness is achieved.

The second proof/rise of the bread before going into the oven!

Indian-Inspired Dahl Soup with Seeded Rye Bread

Lunch

- **Seeded Rye Bread and Indian-Inspired Dahl Soup**
  - o **Lentils:** Contain a rich amount of dietary fiber that will likely push waste and toxins through the body (an excellent detox ingredient). While also containing potassium, which may help reverse the effects of too much salt consumption and lower your blood pressure. Lastly, lentils are versatile; you can sprout them for salads and incorporate them in a cold scoop salad, soups, etc.
  - o **Pumpkin/Sunflower/Carraway seeds:**
    - ▪ **Pumpkin seeds:** May reduce the risk of bladder stones/other urinary issues. And may ease menopause symptoms.
    - ▪ **Sunflower seeds:** Rich in protein and healthy unsaturated fatty acids. Sunflower seeds may lower the risk of heart issues, lower blood pressure, and lower bad cholesterol.
    - ▪ **Carraway seeds:** Specifically used to reduce/prevent digestive problems, heartburn, bloating, gas, loss of appetite, etc.
      - ▪ **Yield:** 4 servings. Each serving = ½ cup dahl and 1-2 oz bread each.

Ingredients:

Dahl (dahl is a very fiber and protein-rich soup, so only a tiny amount at a time is recommended.)
5 cups Veg Stock.
1 cup Green Lentils
3 bay Leaves
1 Tablespoon Olive Oil
1 White Onion, small dice
2 Fresh Garlic Cloves, minced
1 teaspoon Ground Turmeric
½ teaspoon Cayenne Pepper
¼ teaspoon Whole Cumin Seeds
¼ teaspoon Ground Cardamon
½ teaspoon Whole Mustard Seeds
1 teaspoon salt
¼ teaspoon Whole White Peppercorns

Seeded Rye Bread _(great to make the day before or on your meal prep day.)_

1 ½ cups Dark Rye Flour

1 ½ cups Bread Flour

1 teaspoon salt

1 ½ teaspoon Carraway Seeds

2 Tablespoons Raw Pumpkin Seeds

2 Tablespoons Raw Sunflower Seeds

3 Tablespoons Granulated Sugar _(the role of the sugar is to feed/activate the yeast)_

2 teaspoons Active Yeast _(yeast is living bacteria)_

1 ¼ cups Warm Water _(Must be warm to touch. It will kill the yeast if the water feels hot.)_

1 Tablespoon Olive Oil

3 Tablespoons Olive Oil

3 Tablespoon Bread Flour (for dusting)

1 Tablespoon Raw Pumpkin Seeds

1 Tablespoon Raw Sunflower Seeds

Directions:

Dahl

1. Bring the vegetable stock, bay leaves, and lentils to a boil in a medium-sized pot. Reduce to a simmer and cover. Stir occasionally. Cook for 30 minutes or until the lentils are soft.

2. In a pot, add olive oil over medium heat. Add the diced onion and garlic, and sauté until the onions are translucent.

3. Meanwhile, place a sauté pan over medium heat. Add in all the whole seeds and toast until you start and smell the aromatics. Remove from the pan once toasted, so the spices do not burn.

4. Add all the whole toasted species into a spice grinder until they become powder.

5. Add all the fresh ground and pre-ground spices and seasonings to the onions and stir.

6. Once the lentils are soft, remove the bay leaves. Add the lentils and broth into the onion mixture or wise versa. Do not discard leftover broth; we want that included.

7. Use an immersion blender to puree the soup until smooth. Add in more broth if the soup becomes too thick.

8. If you do not have an immersion blender, you can puree the soup in a standing blender in stages. Only blend about 1 cup of the soup at a time.

9. Enjoy!

Seeded Rye Bread

1. Lightly Toast 2 T of sunflower seeds, 2 T of pumpkin seeds, and the caraway seeds in a sauté pan until lightly golden brown. Remove the seeds from the pan to cool.

2. In a standard mixture, add warm water, yeast, 1T oil, and sugar. Stir until frothy.

3. Mix together the flour, toasted seeds, and salt in a large bowl.

4. Using a paddle attachment, slowly add ¾ of the flour mixture. Once combined, add in the rest of the flour mixture. Use a rubber spatula to scrape down the sides of bowls as needed.

5. Once the dough is combined, switch over to a dough hook attachment. Turn the mixture onto medium speed and knead the dough for 9 minutes or until the dough is smooth and elastic. Take the dough out of the bowl and form it into a ball.

6. Coat a large bowl with the oil and place the dough into the bowl. Cover with plastic wrap and place in a warm to rise for 1-2 hours or until the dough doubles.

7. After the dough has risen, lightly punch the dough to release the air.

8. Place the dough on a lightly floured service while using your hands to roll it into a log shape.

9. Spray a bread loaf pan with cooking spray and place the dough into the pan. Sprinkle the dough with the sunflower, gently pumpkin seeds, and press the seeds into the dough. Losing cover with a town or plastic. Let rise for a 30min-1hour or until doubled in size.

   a. *TIP:* If you do not have a bread loaf pan, you can also use a cast-iron skillet, pie plate, oven-safe pan, or sheet pan. This will result in a round bread shape.

10. Preheat oven to 425F.

11. Once risen, remove the covering and bake for 25-40min. Check the bread at 20 min. Cover with foil for the remaining time if the bread is brown to your liking.

12. Let the bread slightly cool, and then remove the bread from the pan. Place the bread on a baking rack. Let the bread completely cool, and then slice.

Cajun Inspired Tilapia with Quinoa Black Bean Salad

Dinner

- **Cajun Inspired Tilapia with Quinoa Black Bean Salad**
  - o **Cucumbers:** Like most fruits and vegetables, cucumbers are high in nutrients while promoting hydration in the body. They also may help with bodyweight goals, promote regular bowel movements, and are very versatile. Cucumbers can be juiced and used in drinks, salads, sauces, and more.
    - ▪ **Yield:** 4 Servings. Each serving = 1 fish fillet and1 cup of salad.

Ingredients:

4, 3oz filets of Tilapia
1 Tablespoon Your favorite Cajun spice blend

Salad *(You can easily make the salad/vinaigrette ahead of time the day or two before to save time the day of)*
1 cup Raw Quinoa
2 cups Vegetable Broth (See Pages 13-15)
1 15oz can of Black Beans, Drained and rinsed.
1 Cucumber peeled and diced.
One cup of Cherry Tomatoes, cut in half.

Vinaigrette
½ cup Olive oil
¼ cup Rice Wine Vinegar
1 Tablespoon Honey
1 teaspoon salt
½ teaspoon Pepper
¼ cup Shallots, minced.
¼ cup Fresh Parsley chopped.

Directions:

1. Place a pot on the stove over high heat. Add in the quinoa and veg broth. Bring to a boil, stir, reduce to a simmer, and cover with a lid. Cook for 20-30 minutes or until the quinoa seeds have formed rings.
2. Remove the cooked quinoa from the pan and place it in a bowl/dish. Put in the fridge to cool.

3. Preheat the oven to 350F.
4. Prepare the vegetables and beans and place them in a bowl.
5. Use a whisk or immersion blender to make the vinaigrette. If using a whisk, slowly drizzle in the oil while whisking.
6. When the Quinoa is cold, place it in the bowl with the veggie mixture and stir in the vinaigrette. Cover and place in the Fridge.
7. Place foil on a sheet pan and spread a thin layer of butter onto the foil.
8. Season both sides of the fish fillets with the Cajun seasoning and place the flat side of the fish down onto the foil.
9. Bake in the oven for 15 minutes or until the fish is flaky and reaches 145F.
10. Enjoy!

Mushroom Fried Rice

- **Mushroom Fried Rice**
  - **Fish Sauce:** Adds an Unami flavor to any dish and does not necessarily transfer a fishy taste. Fish sauce is a good source of iron magnesium and a healthier alternative to salt.

      - **Yield:** 4 Servings. Each serving= is about 1 cup.

Ingredients:

Rice *(make the day before)*
2 cups Raw Brown Rice
4 cups Vegetable Broth (See Pages 13-15)

Marinade/Sauce *(make the day before)*
1 Tablespoon Fresh Ginger, minced
2 Fresh Garlic Cloves, minced
½ bunch of Green Onions, cut on the bias.
1 Tablespoon Fish Sauce
4 Tablespoons Soy Sauce
2 Tablespoon Sweet Chili Sauce

Other
4 Eggs
2 Tablespoons Olive Oil
8oz Mushrooms, sliced.
1-2 Carrots peeled and small diced.
¼ cup Frozen Peas do not thaw.

Garnish- *Optional*
Green Onions
Soy Sauce
Sesame Seeds

Directions:

Day Before
1. Place rice and vegetable broth in a pot. Stir the rice and bring it to a boil. Next, reduce to a simmer, stir again, and cover the pot with a lid.
2. Cook for 20-30 minutes or until the rice is tender.

3. Meanwhile, mix all the ingredients for the marinade together in a container. Cover the container with a lid and place it in the fridge overnight to develop flavor.

4. Cover a sheet pan with parchment paper.

5. Once the rice is done. Place the rice in a single layer on the prepared sheet pan and place it in the fridge overnight with a piece of parchment paper on top. The rice needs air to dry out and cool overnight.

Day Of

6. Place a large sauté pan over medium to high heat. Add the olive oil and all the pan to get hot. Next, sauté the mushrooms and carrots until soft.

7. Meanwhile, whisk the eggs together in a bowl and set them aside.

8. Once the mushrooms and carrots are soft, add the rice to the pan and stir.

9. Now stir in the eggs and allow to cook. Lastly, pour the sauce into the pan and add the frozen peas. Stir and allow to cook. The fried rice is ready when the peas are a bright green color!

Spiced Chai Almond Flour Cookies

Dessert

- **Spiced Chai Almond Flour Cookies**
  - ○ **Almond Flour:** Enriched with vitamin E and many other antioxidants. Almonds may help reduce cancer, diabetes, strokes, and heart disease.
    - ▪ *TIP:* Almond flour is a great alternative GF option when it comes to baking. If you are allergic to nuts, I suggest chickpea four, tapioca flour, or a GF flour blend.
      - ▪ **Yield:** 12-18 Cookies depending on the size of scoop used.

Ingredients:

Tea
1 Black Tea Bag
1 cup Hot Water

Cookies
2 ½ cup Almond Flour
½ teaspoon Baking Soda
½ teaspoon Baking Powder
¼ teaspoon Ground Cloves
1 teaspoon Ground Cinnamon
1/8 teaspoon Ground Allspice
½ teaspoon Ground Ginger
½ teaspoon Salt
4 Tablespoons Coconut Oil, melted
2 teaspoon Vanilla Extract
6 Tablespoons Organic Cane Sugar
½ cup Brewed Black Tea, cooled.

Directions:

1. Preheat the oven to 350F.
2. Place the tea bag into hot water for 10 minutes or until fully brewed. Then place the tea in the fridge to cool.
3. Mix all other ingredients into a bowl.
4. Gently fold in the tea.

5. Prepare a sheet pan with parchment paper and spray the parchment with cooking oil/spray.

6. Use a small cookie scoop and place it on the prepared sheet pan. Leave at least 1 inch between each cookie.

7. Bake for around 15 minutes or until the outside of the cookie is firm to touch.

   a. This is a very wet cookie, so the longer you bake them, the less wet they will become.

8. Allow cookies to cool slightly on the sheet pan. As they start and cool, they will set more (harden).

   a. Allow to set out on the counter to dry out some before putting them in a container.

9. Enjoy. Best eaten the day you make them! Keep refrigerated.

Beverages

- **Green Tea**
- **Vegetable or Chicken Broth**
- **Juice**
- **Water**
- **Any Vitamin Water or Electrolyte Enhanced Water**
  - Electrolytes are essential for staying hydrated and feeling well!
    - Sodium
    - Chloride
    - Magnesium
    - Calcium
    - Potassium

Maintaining Gout

Gout is an illness of tiny crystals and uric acid that form around joints. It causes swelling, redness, irritation, and severe pain.

Cause/Prevention

What Causes Gout?

- o Lifestyle Choices

- o Being overweight

- o Having high blood pressure

- o Eating excessive red meat, animal organs, shellfish, or liquor.

To Prevent and Maintain

- o Consuming plenty of water and fruits heavy in vitamin C will help flush out uric acid.

- o Cherries can reduce flair-ups/gout attacks.

- o Balanced Diet:

  - • Whole grains, lean meats, fruits, vegetables, and low-fat dairy items.

    - ▪ Provides fiber, essential nutrients, and proper digestion.

Menu Ideas for Gout

Breakfast

- **Relieving Apple Smoothie**

○ **Apples:** Layered with malic acid, which helps neutralize uric acid in the bloodstream. Adding apples to your diet may help reduce gout flair-ups and symptoms.

○ **Spirulina:** Blue/green algae that are considered a superfood. Spirulina has many healthy capabilities for almost anyone who experiences discomfort. For example, regular spirulina intake may control blood sugar levels, muscle cramps, suppress oxidation, and more.

  - **Yield:** 2 servings, 12oz each.

Ingredients:

1 Green Apple, peeled, cored, and diced.
½ cup Fresh Spinach; remove or finely chop stems.
1 Fresh Banana
½ cup Fresh or Frozen Peaches
1 teaspoon Spirulina Powder
1 cup Almond Milk, unsweetened
1 teaspoon Fresh Lemon Juice
1 cup Ice

Directions:

1. Place all the ingredients into a blender except the ice. Blend until smooth.
2. Next, add the ice and blend again until the smoothie thickens and is smooth.
3. Enjoy!

Lunch

- **Falafel Meatball Subs on a Whole Grain Baguette topped with a Pickled Slaw.**

- o Garbanzo Beans: Also known as chickpeas, rich in protein, fiber, iron, and phosphorus. They are a fun plant protein option, may help with digestion, and may prevent chronic illnesses.
- **Yield:** 4 Servings. Each serving = 1 hoagie roll filled with 3 falafels, 2 Tablespoons of sauce, and ¼ cup slaw.

Ingredients:

<u>Falafel</u>

1 cup Dried Garbanzo Beans (Chickpeas)
- o *TIP:* Canned garbanzo beans will not result in a crisp/fluffy falafel. The falafels will be too wet and fall apart.
- o Suppose you do not have access to dried beans. Drain/rinse a can of beans and place them between paper towels to dry on the counter for 2 hrs.

½ cup Shallot, diced.

3 Fresh Garlic Cloves

½ bunch Fresh Cilantro

½ bunch Fresh Parsley

¼ teaspoon Ground Cumin

¼ teaspoon Ground Turmeric

½ teaspoon Ground Coriander

¼ teaspoon Cayenne Pepper

¼ teaspoon Salt if canned, ½ teaspoon if dry

¼ teaspoon Pepper

¼ teaspoon Baking Soda *(Baking Soda helps achieve a fluffy texture on the inside of the falafel)*

1 Tablespoon Olive Oil

<u>Venerate Slaw</u>

½ Red Onion

½ cup Carrot

4 Green Onions, cut on the bias

¼ teaspoon Red Pepper Flakes

¼ teaspoon salt

1 Tablespoon Lemon juice

1 Tablespoon Rice wine vinegar

2 Tablespoons Olive Oil

<u>Other Ingredients</u>

4 Honey Wheat Hoagie Rolls

Marinara/Tomato Sauce (See Pages 17-18)

<u>Optional Garnish</u>

Shredded Mozzarella

Directions:

1. Place garbanzo beans in a bowl/dish and cover with water. Soak the beans in water for 24 hours.

   <u>Slaw</u>

2. Cut all the vegetables lengthwise to make very thin strips, about 3 inches long.

3. Whisk together the lemon juice, vinegar, and oil. Pour over veggies and add seasoning.

4. Cover and place in the fridge overnight.

   <u>Falafel</u>

5. Preheat the oven to 400F.

6. Drain the beans and place them on a towel to dry. You can pat them with another towel as well.
7. Place all ingredients for the falafel in a large food processor (if you have a small one, blend in batches).
8. Pulse until crumbs form. Do not blend until smooth.
1. Use a scoop to measure the mixture to make balls. Do not pack down the scoop. Only allow what naturally fits in the scoop for a fluffy product. Repeat
2. Place parchment pepper on a sheet tray and spray with cooking spray.
3. Place the prepared falafel balls on the prepared sheet tray. Drizzle or spray the balls with olive oil.
4. Bake for 20 minutes.
5. You can toast or heat your bread first if desired.
6. Place 3 falafel in each hoagie roll. Drizzle with sauce and top with slaw. Enjoy 😊!

Turkey with a Decant Cherry Sauce, Baked Potato, and Roasted Veggies

Dinner

- **Turkey with a Decant Cherry Sauce, Baked Potato, and Roasted Veggies**
    - o **Cherries:** Have anti-inflammatory compounds that may reduce gout symptoms and flare-ups. They also contain many vitamins and minerals that can boost exercise recovery and may improve your sleep quality.
    - o **Red Potatoes and Their Skin:** I always leave the skins on my potatoes, especially when I make mashed potatoes. The skin adds a depth of flavor and texture contrast. Plus, the skin provides fiber, whereas the potato itself contains Vitamin C. Therefore, they can help you with digestion, repairing body tissue, and providing antitoxins relating to your overall health.
        - ▪ **Yield:** 4 Servings. Each Serving= 4oz turkey, ½ cup veggies, 1 potato, 2oz cherry sauce.

Ingredients:

16oz Turkey Breast
Salt
Pepper
½ teaspoon Dried Italian herbs

Sauce
1 ½ cups Frozen Cherries, pitted and cut in half.
2 Tablespoon Water
½ Tablespoon Cornstarch
1 teaspoon Apple Cider Vinegar
1 Tablespoon Granulated Sugar
Pinch of Salt

Baked Potatoes
4 medium-large Red Potatoes, wash and dry
Olive Oil
Salt

Potato Toppings
Butter
Fresh rosemary, minced.

Salt
White Pepper

Veggies
1 Yellow Squash, sliced in rounds.
1 Yellow Onion thinly sliced.
1 cup Brussel Sprouts, just in half, cut off ends.
½ teaspoon Smoked Paprika.
¼ teaspoon Red Pepper Flakes
½ teaspoon Salt
¼ teaspoon Black Pepper
2 Tablespoons Olive Oil

Directions:

1. Preheat the oven to 400F.
2. Poke each potato with a fork to allow airflow. Next, rub olive oil and salt on each potato and wrap with foil. Place the prepared potatoes on a sheet tray and bake for 20 minutes or until they are tender (if you can easily stab a knife though they are done.
3. Toss veggies, spices, and olive oil on a sheet tray. Spread into a single layer.
4. Bake for 15-20 minutes.
5. Cut the turkey breast(s) into 4 3oz portions. Sprinkle each breast with salt, pepper, and dried herbs.
6. Heat an oven-safe pan over medium heat. Spray with cooking spray and allow to heat up.
7. Sear the turkey breasts on both sides to develop browning. Place in the oven to finish cooking to 165F.
8. Next, mix the cornstarch and lemon juice and set aside. Add all other sauce ingredients into a small pot and bring to a simmer. Slowly whisk in the cornstarch lemon slurry. Simmer until desired thickness is achieved *(sauce coats the back of the spoon)*.
9. Place turkey on your plate with cherry sauce on top, accompanied by the veggies and potatoes.

Zucchini Bread

Dessert:

- **Zucchini Bread**
  - ○ **Zucchini:** Contains antioxidants that are found explicitly in the squash's skin. These antioxidants protect the body against free radicals. Zucchini is also high in water and fiber content which may promote healthy digestion and gut health.
  - ○ _TIP: Corn starch has two main factors in bread. One, it helps achieve a fluffy sponge, and two, it helps suck up some of the water from the zucchini._
    - ▪ Yield: 1 loaf, 4oz slice (about 1-2 inches thick) or each serving.

Ingredients:

2 eggs
½ cup Granulated Cane Sugar
½ cup Coconut Oil, melted
2 teaspoon Vanilla Extract
1 ½ cups Grated Zucchini (do not drain liquid.)

Flour Mixture
1 cup All-Purpose Flour
½ cup Whole Wheat Flour
2 Tablespoons Corn Starch
½ teaspoon Ground Flaxseed
½ teaspoon Baking Powder
½ teaspoon Baking Soda
½ teaspoon Salt
¼ teaspoon Ground All Spice
½ teaspoon Ground Cinnamon

Directions:

1. Preheat oven to 325F.
2. Use the whisk attachment on a standard mixer. _(You can also use a handheld mixer or just a hand whisk/wooden spoon.)_
3. Add the eggs and sugar into the bowl and cream together.
4. Next, add the oil, vanilla, and zucchini. Mix until well combined.
5. Slowly add the flour mixture. ¼ at a time. Mix on low speed.

6. Mix until all the flour is combined. Do not over-mix, or the bread may become dense.
7. Spray a bread loaf pan with cooking spray. _TIP:_ If your pan is well-used (old). It may be beneficial if you coat the inside of the pan with a light layer of flour after spraying it.
8. Pour the batter into the prepared bread loaf pan and bake for 45-60 minutes or until the bread is cooked through the center. Check the center with a butter knife or toothpick.
9. After cooling, place in an airtight container and keep in the fridge.

Beverages

- **Fruit juices**
- **Water**
- **Any Vitamin Water or Electrolyte Enhanced Water**

Information on Eating Disorders

- **What is an Eating Disorder?** A wide range of phycological conditions may cause irregular eating patterns. These irregular eating patterns can lead to an eating disorder and significant health consequences. Irregular eating patterns could be caused by an individual punishing themself for doing something wrong, seeing themselves as a bad person, seeing themselves as overweight, or even losing weight.

- **Development of an Eating Disorder:**
  - *Genetics:* Experts believe that eating disorders can be hereditary.
    - Experts have also suggested that the brain structure and biology of the body may play a role in eating disorder development.
  - *Personality traits:* Neuroticism, perfectionism, and impulsivity are linked to having a higher risk of eating disorders.
  - The pressure comes from the media of being "thin" or "skinny."

- **6 Most Common Types**
  - *Anorexia:* The illness of viewing oneself as overweight, even severely underweight. Anorexia results in limiting food intake and purging.
  - *Bulimia:* The disease of eating unregular large amounts of food and then purging.
  - *Binge Eating:* Binding includes having a lack of control when eating and shaming themselves. This illness does not involve purging.
  - *PICA:* Eating non-food items, such as chalk dirt. Soap, etc. this illness is mainly developed in children, pregnant women, and individuals with mental disorders.
  - *Rumination:* Individuals who regurgitate the food they ate no earlier than 30 minutes prior.
  - *Avoidant/Resistant Food Intake:* The lack of interest in certain foods because of their taste/smell/appearance. This individual may only eat one food item, for example, chicken nuggets.

- **Hurtful Myths and Stereotypes**
  - Lifestyle choice
  - A diet that went too "far."

o It only occurs in adolescent females.

o You can tell if someone has an eating disorder by their appearance.

o Purging is an effective way to lose weight.

- These myths are misleading and may even lead to more people developing eating disorders. These myths also may make it harder for individuals to recover from their illnesses.

- People of any age, any gender, and any shape or size can have or develop an eating disorder. It is not our right to judge anymore by how they eat or look on the outside because we do not know what they are going through as individuals.

- **Recovery Process and Programs**
  o Every individual will have different levels of an illness, different medical/illness history, and different goals/diagnoses.
    - Therefore, it can take several weeks, months, or even years for the individual to fully heal from their illness.
  o It is essential that if you think someone is experiencing any of the symptoms I listed above, you reach out to your nearest eating recovery center and ask what the next steps are.

- **Programs Offered:** Every facility will do things slightly differently, but here are some general programs and processes.
  o Outpatient, inpatient, residential, hospitalized, intensive outpatient treatment, and more.
  o The individuals will go through a series of groups, programs, one-on-one seasons, therapy, support systems, and meal plans. They will have support from the staff at the facility to work through their fears, struggles, goals, and illness.

- **Statistics:**
  o "Eating disorders are among the deadliest mental illnesses. In fact, 10,200 deaths each year are the direct result of an eating disorder." (ANAD, 2021).
  o So please get your loved ones or anyone with an eating disorder the help they need.

My Go-To at Home Meals

Breakfast on the Go

- **Chia Seed Pudding**

○ **Chia Seeds**: High in fiber, high in protein, and are enriched with healthy fats like omega 3's!

- **Yield**: 4 servings. The standard serving size of chia seeds is 2 Tablespoons.

Ingredients:

8 Tablespoons Chia Seeds
2 cups Almond or Soy Milk
2 teaspoons Vanilla extract
1 teaspoon Stevia Powder
½ teaspoon Ground Cinnamon

Toppings *(Optional: Anything you like or have in the kitchen.)*
Pecans
Diced Apples
Berries

Directions:

1. Place 4 containers in front of you. *(1 container = 1 serving)*
2. Pour ½ cup of milk into each container. Followed by 2 Tablespoons of chia seeds, ½ teaspoon of vanilla, ¼ teaspoon of stevia, and ¼ teaspoon of

cinnamon in each container. Lightly stir the chia seeds/other ingredients throughout the milk. Cover the containers with lids or plastic wrap.

3. Place in your fridge and chill until the pudding is thick.
4. Once the pudding is set, top it with nuts and fresh fruit.
5. Enjoy!

- **Muesli** (See Pages 65-66)
- **Nut Bar**
- **Banana Or Other Fruits**
- **Coffee Protein Shake**

- **Coffee Protein Shake**

Who doesn't want a way to have their coffee and breakfast in one? Especially someone on the go!

- **Yield:** 2 12oz servings

Ingredients:

¾ cup Cold Brew Coffee
1/3 cup Almond Milk, unsweetened
1 Scoop of your favorite Nutritional Protein Powder *(low glycemic index)*
½ Banana (I use frozen)
½ teaspoon Vanilla Syrup or Carmel, plus more for garnish
1 cup Ice

Directions:

1. Place all ingredients into the blender except the ice and banana. Blend until smooth
2. Now add the ice and blend until smooth and thickened.
3. Pour into a travel cup and enjoy!

Packed Lunches

- **Salad Kits from The Store!**
- **Yogurt With Homemade Granola**
  - ○ **Granola**

- **Pine Nuts:** High in protein and antioxidant levels. Specifically, pine nuts contain iron and magnesium, which help sustain energy levels. They also are enriched with Vitamin C, which may help your skin's health.
- **Flaxseed:** A bold, nutty, and earthy flavored seed complements granola nicely with great health benefits. At the same time, we are getting a boost of fiber and fatty acids from the flaxseeds. Consuming flaxseeds regularly may improve digestion, lower blood pressure, and may even help cholesterol levels.

- **Side Note:** You can make a flax egg when baking a vegan cake or bread! Mix 1 Tablespoon ground flaxseed with 3 Tablespoons of water to create one egg replacer.

- **Yield:** About 4 cups. ¼ to ½ cup per serving.

Ingredients:

2 cups Whole Oats
¼ cup Raw Pine Nuts
¼ cup Raw Slivered Almonds.
¼ cup Dried Apricots, chopped.
¼ cup Dried Blueberries
1 Tablespoon Ground flaxseed or 1 ½ Tablespoons of ground Trilogy mix (flax, chia, hemp)
½ teaspoon Salt
¼ teaspoon Ground Cinnamon
1 teaspoon Vanilla Extract
¼ cup Whiskey Thai Honey or any Honey you have on hand
¼ cup Coconut Oil, melted

Directions:

1. Preheat oven to 350F.
2. Place parchment paper on 1-2 sheet pans.
3. In a large bowl, combine all the dry ingredients. Then stir in the wet ingredients (melted coconut oil and honey).
4. Spread the granola mixture onto the prepared pan(s). Make sure the granola is in a single layer and not stacked.
5. Bake for 20-25 minutes and stir the granola halfway through cook time.
6. Allow the granola to cool before placing it in bags/containers.

- **Sandwiches**
  - Turkey sandwich *(see page 52)* with chips and veggies dipped in ranch or peanut butter, depending on my mood!
  - Breakfast Sandwich/Bowl
  - PB&J

- **Leftovers!**

Dinners at Home

- **Soups**
  - o Soups are something I can whip together quickly if I do not know what else to make. The great thing about soups is you can throw pretty much anything into the pot that needs to be used up in the pantry and fridge.

  - o **Ham and Vegetable Soup**

  - ▪ The combination of onions, carrots, and celery is the standard *mirepoix* (the foundation of flavor) of most soups and sauces. You can even create a mirepoix bed to cook meat on top of in the oven.

  - ▪ **Tri-Colored Carrots:** (Purple, White, Orange) Specifically, purple carrots may reduce inflammation, help achieve weight loss goals, and reduce the risk of chronic illness/diseases.
  - ▪ Kale: The leafy green that some people may avoid because of the bitter notes it contains. I find that if you add enough flavor (spices) and mix the greens with other ingredients, the natural flavor of kale advances, and the bitter notes go away.
  - • Kale: A very nutrient-dense vegetable with many benefits for the body and mind. Kale is loaded with vitamins and powerful antioxidants. It is remarkably high in vitamins C, K, B, and more. Lastly, it may help reduce cholesterol and blood pressure and helps with many functions in the body.
    - ▪ **Yield:** 4 12oz bowls

Ingredients:

2 Tablespoons Butter or Olive Oil

1 White Onion

½ cup baby Tricolor Carrots, 1 of each color (*who knew colorful carrots could add such a flavor and appearance enhancer, compared to your boring everyday orange carrot.*)

2 Celery stalks

1 cup Fresh Kale, chopped

½ teaspoon Dried Thyme

½ teaspoon Salt

¼ teaspoon Black Pepper

1 teaspoon Turmeric

¼ teaspoon Smoked paprika (*I love the aroma of smoked paprika and that flavor punch it brings to a dish*)

2 Tablespoons All-Purpose Flour. (*If you are avoiding gluten/wheat, you can use a corn starch slurry instead, like see on the page 42*)

32oz Vegetable broth (*see pages 13-15*)

2 Red Potatoes, washed, small dice, skin on

1 cup white beans (*I like to add beans for a little extra protein, fiber, flavor, and textural contrast.*)

16oz Diced Ham.

3 Bay Leaves

½ cup Half & Half

Directions:

1. Place a large pot over medium heat on the stove. Add in the butter.
2. Small dice onions, carrots, celery, and kale. Place them into the pot. Stir and allow them to sauté for a few minutes or until the onions are translucent.
3. Stir in all the spices and Sautee until they become aromatic.
4. Stir in the flour and cook for another 1-2 minutes or until the flour is golden. Do not allow the flour to burn.
5. Slowly whisk in the vegetable broth to avoid clumps.
6. Bring to a boil and add the potatoes once boiling reduces to a simmer. Next, stir in the beans, ham, and bay leaves. Cook for 20 minutes so the potatoes can become tender, and so the soup will develop flavor.
7. Remove the bay leaves and stir in half and half. Lightly simmer for a few more minutes and enjoy.

Ramen with Tofu, Green Onions, and Seaweed

- o **Elevated Instant Ramen**

  (Ramen with Tofu, Green Onions, and Seaweed)
  - ▪ As most household ramen is always kept in my house! Especially since my husband does not like to cook, ramen and eggs are his go-to's.
  - ▪ **Tofu:** Made from condensed soy milk pressed into a block, similar to cheese making. Tofu is high in protein, contains all the essential amino acids and nutrients, and is filled with beneficial isoflavones. Isoflavones may help with heart health digestion, reduces the risk of diabetes, and reduces the risk of cancers.

      - ▪ **Yield:** 4-6 Servings

Ingredients:

4 Instant Ramen Noodle Packets.

6-8 cups Vegetable Broth (See Pages 13-15); the *amount of veg broth depends on how much liquid you like in your ramen.*

1, 14oz Firm Tofu Package, drain the liquid, and small dice the tofu.

½ teaspoon Red Pepper Flakes *(optional)*

1 bunch of Green Onions (scallions), cut on the bias.

4 Small Dry Sheets of Seaweed, garnish

Directions:

1 Place a large pot over high heat. Add in the vegetable broth and bring to a boil.
2 Add in the noodles, tofu, and green onions. Stir so the noodles spread apart.
3 Reduce the heat to a simmer.
4 Next, add in two seasoning packets, stir and cover with a lid. Allow to cook for 3-5minutes or until the noodles are cooked, the tofu is heated through, and the flavor has developed.

   (I only add in two seasoning packets to reduce the sodium levels. The vegetable broth and dried seaweed are also flavor and nutrient enhancers). *TIP: you can save the other two seasoning packets and use them in a different pasta dish.*
5 Evenly distribute into 4 bowls and top with a sheet of seaweed.

Beef Hard Shell Tacos with All the Fixings

- **Tacos**
  - **Beef Hard Shell Tacos with All the Fixings!**
  - **Beef:** Red meat contains a large amount of L-Carnitine. L-Carnitine is an amino acid that helps transport fat in our bodies. Fats must be transported for general health and weight management.
    - **Yield:** 4 Servings. Each serving= 2 tacos. Each taco gets 2 oz meat, 2 Tablespoons guacamole, and 1 Tablespoon of each fixing.

Ingredients:

Beef Filling
1lb ground beef
½ teaspoon Salt
¾ teaspoon Cumin
¼ teaspoon Smoked Paprika.
½ teaspoon Chili powder
¼ teaspoon Coriander
¼ teaspoon Red Pepper Flakes

Fixings
Black olives, sliced.
Diced tomato.
Shredded Colby Jack Cheese

Guacamole
2 Ripe Avocados
½ Bunch Fresh Cilantro, chopped
1 Small Jalapeno, minced.
¼ teaspoon Garlic powder
¼ teaspoon Salt
1/8 teaspoon Pepper
1 Tablespoon Fresh lime juice
8 Hard Taco Shells

Directions:

1. Preheat the oven to 350F.
2. Place a large pan over medium heat.
3. Add the grown beef to the pan and allow it to brown.
4. Meanwhile, mash avocados in a bowl with a fork. Stir in the rest of the ingredients and set aside.
5. Once the meat is browned, drain any grease that is in the pan.
6. Next, stir in all the spices and 1 Tablespoon of water to the meat. Reduce to low heat.
7. Place the hard-shell tacos in the oven on a sheet tray for 5-10 minutes.
8. While the shells are in the oven, you can cut/prepare all the fixings.
9. Assemble your tacos!

Shrimp Soft Tacos with a Mango Salsa

- **Shrimp Soft Tacos with a Mango Salsa**
  - Mangos: Have a long list of antioxidants. Some of the nutrients that people are getting after eating mangoes are the immune-busting vitamins such as VA.

    - **Yield:** 4 Servings. Each serving = 2 tacos. Each taco gets 2oz shrimp, ½ teaspoon sauce, and 2 Tablespoons salsa.

Ingredients:

16oz Shrimp, deveined.
½ teaspoon Garlic Powder
¼ teaspoon Smoked Paprika
1 teaspoon Dried Italian Herb Blend
¼ teaspoon Black Pepper
½ teaspoon Salt
8 small Flour Tortillas

Salsa
1 Fresh Mango
½ bunch Fresh Cilantro
½ Jalapeno, minced.
½ Red Onion, small diced
¼ teaspoon Salt
1 teaspoon Lime Juice

Sauce
½ cup Ranch Dressing
1-2 Chipotle Peppers in Adobo Sauce, include some of the sauce
2-3 Tablespoons Fresh Cilantro

Garnish
Avocado
Lime Wedge

Directions:

<u>Shrimp</u>

1. Peel and remove the tails from the shrimp.
2. In a small bowl, mix the spice blend.
3. Place a large pan over medium heat. add 1 Tablespoon Olive oil
4. Add Shrimp to the pan and evenly sprinkle the shrimp with the spice blend. You will only use about half the spice blend.
5. Stir and cook the shrimp until they turn pink.
6. Place the tortillas in the microwave for 10 seconds to warm.

<u>Salsa</u>

7. _Peel the mango. Cut a square around the mango, leaving the giant pit in the center. Then small dice the mango flesh.
8. Place the mango in a bowl with all the other salsa ingredients and stir.

<u>Sauce</u>

9. Puree/blend all ingredients until smooth.
10. Assemble your tacos!

Bacon, Caramelized
Onion, and Cheese
Quiche

- **Quiche**
  - o My husband is obsessed with eggs! So, we like to make breakfast for dinner now and then.
  - o **Bacon, Caramelized Onion, and Cheese Quiche**
    - o **Rye flour:** High in fiber and has many nutrient properties. It depends on how much Rye flour is used and how many health benefits you get from it.
      - ▪ Rye flour is a whole grain that takes longer to process in your body than white flour. Thus, rye flour may make you feel fuller sooner and for a more extended period. It also is one of the best choices for people with diabetes because of its low glycemic index.
    - o Eggs: Layered with choline, lutein, zeaxanthin, omega 3's, and protein, they commonly do not affect blood cholesterol. Choline is a needed nutrient to build cell membranes and is related to brain functions. Lastly, lutein and zeaxanthin are related to eye health.
      - o **Yield:** 1 pie dough/1 quiche= 4 Servings.

Ingredients:

3-2-1 Pie Dough
- o *TIPS:(when making your pie dough, you can achieve a much flakier and flavorful crust than store-bought)*
  - ▪ This recipe is super easy.
  - ▪ You can make the pie dough the night before or a couple of days in advance. You just wrap the prepared dough in plastic wrap and place it in the fridge.
    - • Let dough come to room temperature for 3-5 minutes before rolling out.
  - ▪ The colder the ingredients, the flaky the crust will be.
  - ▪ Do not over-mix or roll the dough. The more you touch the dough, the better chance for a dense and less flaky crust.
  - ▪ You must use a scale to weigh out the flour and butter. The recipe will not work with measuring cups.
  - ▪ Double this recipe if you make a pie that requires a top crust.

3oz Rye Flour and 3oz All-Purpose Flour = 6oz flour

4oz Cold Unsalted Stick Butter

½ teaspoon Salt

2oz Cold Water (use a measuring cup)

Filling

6 Eggs

2 Tablespoons 2% Milk

½ teaspoon Paprika

½ teaspoon Salt

1 White/Yellow Onion thinly sliced.

4-6 Strips of bacon

8oz Shredded Cheese of your choice

¼ teaspoon Black Pepper

¼ teaspoon Ground Cumin

½ teaspoon Dried Thyme

Directions:

1. Preheat the oven to 375F.

   3-2-1 Pie Dough

2. In a bowl, add the flour and salt.

3. Cut the butter into small dice and fold/mix it into the flour mixture with a pastry cutter, fork, or your hands. You want the butter to be about pea-sized, no smaller.

4. Use a wooden spoon to gently fold the cold water into the flour-butter mixture. Allow the ingredients to barely come together. If the dough is dry, you can get more water. You do not want the dough to be wet, though.

5. Form the dough into a thick/flat circle, wrap the dough in plastic wrap, and place it in the fridge.

Filling

6. Place a medium-sized pan over medium heat. Place the bacon in the pan and cook for 3 minutes on each side or until desired crispness is achieved.

7. Place bacon on a paper towel and set it aside. Cut bacon into small pieces.

8. Use the same pan to caramelize the onions. If there is too much grease or burned bacon bits, you can wipe out the pan.

9. Leave some grease in the pan for the onions, though.

10. Add the onions to the pan over medium heat. Cook the onions for several minutes before stirring. Your instinct may be to stir, but it is best just to walk away to let the magic happen in the pan when caramelizing onions. After the first stir, add the pepper, cumin, and thyme. Stir again and walk away.

11. If the onions start to brown/burn, stir and reduce the heat.
12. Meanwhile, whisk the eggs in a bowl with milk, salt, and paprika. Whisk for a few minutes to bring a lot of air into the eggs.
13. When the onions are translucent and caramelized, remove them from the heat and set them aside.
14. Bring the dough out of the fridge and unwrap it.
15. Lightly dust the counter with flour.
16. Place the dough on the floured surface and use a rolling pin to roll the dough out into a circle.
17. The best way to test if the dough is rolled out enough is by Turing your pie plate upside down and holding it over the rolled dough. If the dough is an inch or two wider than the pie plate, then the dough is rolled out enough.
18. Place the rolled-out dough into the pie plate and gently press the dough into the creases of the pan to get out any air pockets.
19. You can fold or crimp the top edges of the crust.
20. Next, place the onions and bacon evenly on the bottom of the pie. Top with the cheese and pour the egg mixture on top.
21. Place the pie plate on a sheet pan and place it in the oven for 45-55 minutes. Use a toothpick or butter knife to test if the center of the egg is cooked through.
22. Allow the quiche to cool slightly before slicing. Use a serrated knife.
23. Enjoy!

Chicken Parmesan with Broccoli Salad and Alfredo Pasta

- **Chicken Parmesan with Broccoli Salad and Alfredo Pasta**
  - **Parmesan:** A magical cheese low in fat, lactose-free, and has a salty/nutty flavor. Plus, parmesan may help your bone health and contains an easily digestible protein (contains all essential amino acid proteins).
  - **Broccoli:** Different preparations of vegetables will result in different nutrients being produced/highlighted. For example, when you stir fry/cook broccoli, it reduces the amount of vitamin C in the vegetable. Both cooked and raw broccoli is still very nutritious, though!
    - With regular intake, broccoli may reduce inflammation, protect general health, contain high amounts of fiber (help control blood sugar levels), support healthy digestion (relieving constipation), support brain function health, and much more.
      - **Yield:** 4 Servings. Each serving= 3oz chicken, 2oz sauce, ½ cup pasta, 1 cup salad.

Ingredients:

Pasta
¾ cup All-Purpose Flour
½ cup Rye Flour
¼ cup Semolina Flour
½ teaspoon salt
2 Eggs
1 Tablespoon Olive Oil
¼ cup Water

Chicken *(if you want tomato sauce on top, see pages 17-18)*
4, 3 to 4-oz Chicken Breasts
Salt & Pepper
1 egg
½ cup All-Purpose Flour
1 cup Italian Herbed Breadcrumbs; if *you only have plain breadcrumbs at home, add dried Italian herbs.*
Vegetable Oil

Toppings:
Shredded Parmesan

Alfredo Sauce

1 Tablespoon Stick Butter

2 Fresh Garlic Cloves, minced

1 cup Half & Half

1 cup 2% Milk

1 cup Grated Parmesan.

1 cup shredded parmesan

¼ teaspoon Salt

¼ teaspoon Pepper

Salad *(I cheat and use the broccoli salad kit at the store)*

1 Small Head of Fresh Broccoli, cut into small florets. Cut stems into thin/short strips.

1 Bag Coleslaw Mix (purple & green cabbage, shredded carrots, etc.)

2 Tablespoons Sunflower Seeds

2 Tablespoons Dried Cranberries

Dressing of Choice

Directions:

Pasta

1. Mix flours and salt. Create a well in the center of the flour.
2. Add the eggs and oil to the well. Gently start folding the flour over the eggs to form a dough ball. If the dough is dry, fold in the water.

3. The dough should be sticky to the touch.

4. On a lightly floured surface, knead the dough for a few minutes.

5. Allow dough to rest for 10 minutes. Meanwhile, set up your pasta machine.

6. Cut the pasta dough into small sections, flatten, and feed the dough through a pasta machine with flour until almost paper-thin. Then feed the thin dough through the fettuccine noodle cutter.

7. If you do not have a pasta machine or cutter. Roll the dough out about ¼ inch thick and cut into strips.

   a. *TIP: You can make these noodles 2-4 days in advance to save time on the day of this meal. Place the cut noodles in a flat layer*

    b. *in a container. Place parchment paper on top and add another layer of noodles. Sprinkle some flour on each layer to help prevent sticking—repeat and seal the container with a lid and place it in the fridge.*

8. Boil the fresh-cut noodles in salted water for 2-4 minutes or until al dente.

9. Drain the water and drizzle the noddle with olive oil so they do not stick.

Chicken

10. Prepare a standard breading procedure. Place three bowls, plates, or dishes in front of you. In the first bowl, on the left, place the flour. In the middle bowl, whisk the egg with a splash of water. In The third bowl, place the breadcrumbs.

11. If the chicken breasts are thick, butterfly them in half.

12. Place a large pan over medium heat. Pour a thin layer of vegetable oil into the bottom of the pan.

13. Season each piece of chicken with salt and pepper.

14. Place the seasoned chicken in the flour first, then the egg, and lastly, in the breadcrumbs. Set aside on a plate. Repeat.

    a. *Tip:* Make sure the whole piece of chicken is evenly coated in the flour, then evenly coated in egg, and lastly, evenly coated in breadcrumbs for the best results.

15. When the oil is heated in the pan, place each breaded chicken breast in the oil. Flip over the chicken when the first side is golden brown—Cook to an internal temperature of 165F.

16. Top with parmesan.

Sauce

17. In a saucepan/small pot, melt the butter. Add in the minced garlic and sauté until you smell the garlic cooking.

18. Stir the garlic around and whisk in the milk and half & half.

19. Bring to a simmer and slowly whisk the parmesan, salt, and pepper.

20. Simmer until you reach desired thickness. (Do not boil)

21. If the sauce does not thicken enough, you can add a cornstarch slurry.

22. You can toss the noodles in the Alfredo sauce or just put it on top.

Salad

23. Toss all the prepared ingredients together.

Hillary's Stuffed Pretzel Burger

- **Hillary's Stuffed Pretzel Burgers and Fries**
  - Mushrooms: A touchy ingredient for some people because of the mushroom's flavor/texture. I love the fungi, both raw and cooked! There are many different types of mushrooms in the world, and they are very versatile ingredients. *(Mushrooms can be used for sauces, soups, vegetarian burgers, and more)*
    - Mushrooms contain beta-glucan, reducing your cholesterol and improving your heart health. They also have copper, which triggers your body to make red blood cells. The red blood cells are used to deliver oxygen throughout your body.
      - **Yield:** 4 Servings.

Ingredients:

1lb Ground Beef
4 Pretzel buns

Filling
2oz Fresh Mushrooms, small chop
½ White Onion, small dice
1 (packed) cup Fresh Spinach
1 teaspoon Dried Italian Herbs
2 slices of cheese

Burger Seasoning
¼ teaspoon Salt
1/8 teaspoon Black Pepper
½ teaspoon Ground Coriander
¼ teaspoon Ground Cumin

Sauce
½ cup Ranch Dressing
1-2 Chipotle Peppers in Adobo Sauce, include some of the sauce
2-3 Tablespoons Fresh Cilantro

Optional Toppings
Cheese
Lettuce
Tomato

½ bag Frozen French fries

Directions:

1 Preheat the Oven or Air fryer to 400F.

2 Preheat the Grill or Cast-iron Pan.

3 Place a small pan over medium heat. Add 1 Tablespoon of olive oil.

4 Add in the mushrooms, onions, and dried herbs. Sauté for 3 minutes. Sprinkle with salt and pepper to taste. Add the spinach and continue to sauté until the onions are translucent and the spinach is wilted.

5 Separate the ground beef into 4 sections. Flatten the meat into 4 thin patties. Each patty should be around 4 oz.

6 Take 2 slices of cheese and tear each in half. Fold each half in half again.

7 Place each folded half slice of cheese onto the center of each meat patty.

8 Place 2 Tablespoons of veggies mixture on top of the cheese in each patty.

9 Fold the meat patties over the filling, creating a ball. Flatten out into a thick stuffed patty. Try and make sure all the filling is covered by meat.

10 Mix the burger seasoning and evenly sprinkle onto both sides of each patty.

11 Place your frozen fries into the air fryer for about 10 minutes or your oven for about 10-15 minutes.

12 Spray your Grill or cast-iron pan with oil/cooking spray.

13 Grill each side for 4-8minutes, depending on how you like your meat cooked. *(Only flip the burgers once for best results.)* Allow the burgers to rest on a plate for a few minutes.

14 Puree the adobo peppers and cilantro into the ranch.

15 You can toast the buns in a hot skillet with butter or olive oil. Or brush the buns with olive oil and toast on the grill.

16 Place 2 Tablespoons of chipotle ranch sauce on the bottom of the pretzel bun, place burger on top, and other optional toppings. Serve with fries, and enjoy.

Baked Spaghetti

- **Baked Spaghetti**
  - One of my mom's go-to dishes when I was growing up. This is an easy recipe and can be a little time-consuming, so plan for that.
  - This hearty casserole dish is perfect for adding to your winter comfort food list. This recipe makes a large amount, so it is excellent for having a lot of leftovers or for a big gathering! You can also freeze portioned-out leftovers and pull them out whenever you do not feel like cooking *(Thaw in the fridge overnight for the best re-heating results)*.
  - *Easy to make a day or two ahead of time and then put in the oven before dinner. Bring the dish to room temp and uncover before putting the casserole into the oven.*
  - **Black Olives:** High in Vitamin E and other antioxidants. Olives have many health benefits, such as heart health. They also contain healthy fats extracted to make olive oil used in the Mediterranean diet. Olive oil promotes healthy eating/living and may help with weight loss when replacing unhealthy fats with olive oil.
    - **Yields:** 10-12 Servings.

Ingredients:

12oz Spaghetti Noodles

1lb Ground Beef *(you can leave the beef out for a vegetarian dish or even replace it with chicken.)*

1 medium-large Yellow Onion, diced

1 Green Bell Pepper, diced

4oz Fresh Sliced Mushrooms

1 Tablespoon Olive Oil

1 28 oz can Diced Tomatoes, undrained

1 2.25oz can Slice Black Olives, drained

1 teaspoon Dried Oregano

1 teaspoon dried Italian herb blend

¼ teaspoon Salt

¼ teaspoon Black Pepper

½ teaspoon Ground Coriander

2 cups Shredded Cheese

1 10.5 oz can Condensed Cream of Mushroom Soup, undiluted

¼ cup Water

¼ cup Grated Parmesan Cheese

Directions:

1. Preheat the oven to 350F
2. Heat a large pot of water over high heat. Sprinkle salt *(about 1 Tablespoon)* in the water and bring to a boil.
3. Heat a large skillet/pan over medium-high heat. Crumble the ground beef into the pan and cook until browned. Remove any grease that forms in the pan.
4. Once the water is boiling, add in the noodles, stir, reduce the heat, and cook until the noodles are al dente. *(Have a bite, not completely soft).* Drain and rinse the cooked noodles under cold water. Toss the noodles with a drizzle of olive oil and set them aside.
5. Remove cooked beef from the pan and set it aside.
6. In the same pan over medium-high heat, add 1 Tablespoon of olive oil and prepare fresh veggies. Sautee until they are soft.
7. Once the veggies are soft, add the ground beef back into the pan, along with the olives, diced tomatoes/juice, oregano, salt, black pepper, coriander, and Italian seasoning. Stir until combined and lightly simmer for 5 minutes.
8. Mix the mushroom soup with water until smooth.
9. Grease a 13inch baking dish. Place half the spaghetti noodles in the bottom of the pan. Evenly distribute half the meat/veggie mixture over the noodles. Sprinkle with 1 cup of shredded cheese—repeat layers.
10. Pour the soup mixture on top of the final layer and then sprinkle with parmesan.
11. Bake uncovered for 30-35 minutes. Or until the edges are bubbling, and the casserole is heated to 165F.
12. Enjoy!

Desserts

- (My biggest downfall is 100% desserts. I have a big, sweet tooth. So, I try choosing healthier dessert options. Like those brownies under the diabetic dessert options.)
- **Ice cream, dark chocolate, cookies, brownies, fresh fruit, etc.**
- **Bourbon Chocolate Mousse**

- **Bourbon Chocolate Mousse**
  - *If I want to be fancy or if we are having guests over, sometimes I will make this scrumptious mousse.*
  - ***Dark Chocolate:*** Contains less milk and sugar than milk/white chocolate. Dark Chocolate may also have many health benefits, such as improving blood flow, lowering blood pressure, protecting LDL from oxidation, containing antioxidants, and more.

    - **Yield:** 4 Servings.

Ingredients:

Base
6.5oz Dark Chocolate Chunks
1.5 Tablespoon Unsweetened Cocoa Powder
1/2 Tablespoon Granulated Sugar
Pinch of Salt

Fluff
2-3 Tablespoon Bourbon
1 ½ cups Heaving Whipping Cream
1 teaspoon Vanilla Extract
2 Tablespoons Powdered Sugar
TIP: To stabilize your whipped cream/mousse, you can add ¼ teaspoon Cream of Tartar

Garnish
Powdered Sugar
Fresh Cherrie/Fruit/Berries

Directions:

1 Place the fluff ingredients in a standard mixer and whip for several minutes until stiff peaks are achieved.
2 Place all the base items into a microwave-safe bowl.
3 Microwave for 30 seconds, stir and repeat until the chocolate mixture is smooth. Microwave in short increments so the chocolate does not burn.
4 Gently fold the whipped cream into the chocolate with a rubber spatula until combined and smooth.
5 Place into dessert cups and enjoy!

Snacks

- **Mixed Nuts/Seeds**
- **Veggies and Dip**
- **Chips or Crackers**
- **Granola**
- **Fresh fruit**
- **Dark Chocolate**

<u>*Drinks/Beverages*</u>

- *My family stays away from sodas, energy drinks, and other artificial drinks. However, we do splurge on sweet tea and occasional alcoholic drinks.*

- ○ **Water**
- ○ **Vitamin/Electrolyte Waters**
- ○ **Sweet Tea**
- ○ **Hot Tea/Coffee**
    - ▪ **Tea**: Herbal Tea and black tea can improve your gut health. There are many different bacteria in your gut. Most bacteria are needed for your health and immune system, and some are not. The tea may be able to flush out harmful bacteria.

- Herbal teas also have natural healing properties in them may help with your metabolism, and some teas have natural caffeine.
  - **Coffee:** The caffeine enters your bloodstream and travels to your brain when consuming coffee. Once the caffeine enters your brain, it will give you energy and may improve brain function, memory, and moods over time. This may surprise some people, but coffee also contains Vitamins B, manganese, and potassium.
    - Coffee thus improves your physical performance, mood, and movement to reduce the risk of several conditions, such as cancer, strokes, and Parkinson's.
- **Moscow Mules**
- **Hard Seltzers**
- **Sour Beers**
- **Wine**

Party Foods

- **Cranberry Meatballs**

o I have been making these meatballs for years, and my friends love them. It may seem like a strange combo but do not knock it till you try it!

o **Cranberries:** Many health-boosting benefits, such as helping eyesight, may reduce the risk of urinary tract infections, may reduce chances for liver disease, and may improve gut health

- **Yield:** 8-12 Servings, 3-5 meatballs each.

Ingredients:

2 lb. (32oz) Frozen Meatballs

Sauce
1 14oz can cranberry sauce (jellied or with whole cranberries)
1 cup Ketchup
2 Tablespoons Brown Sugar
2 Tablespoons Worcestershire Sauce
1 Tablespoon Lemon Juice

Directions:

1. Preheat the oven to 425F
2. Place the frozen meatballs on a sheet tray and bake for 20 minutes or until heated through.
3. Meanwhile, place a saucepan over medium-high heat. Add in all the sauce ingredients.
4. Whisk the sauce items to combine and bring to a gentle bowl.
5. Once the meatballs are done, remove them from the oven and place them into a crockpot or baking/travel dish. Pour the sauce over the meatballs

and stir to coat evenly. Keep warm in the slow cooker or a low-temperature oven until the party starts.

6. Enjoy!

- **Spinach Artichoke Wonton Cups**

o **Artichokes:** Loaded with dietary fiber, folate, magnesium, potassium, iron, and more. Artichokes are a versatile ingredient and are a great after work out a snack for recovering and fueling your muscles. *(You can put artichokes on pizza, in a salad dressing, in a dip, in a sauce, and more.)*

- **Yield:** 12 servings = 2 cups each.

Ingredients:

24 Wonton Wrappers

Filling
8oz Fresh Spinach
3oz Fresh Chopped Kale
½ teaspoon Lemon Juice
8oz jar Artichoke Hearts, drained and chopped
5oz Cream Cheese, room temp
½ cup Sour Cream
¾ cup Shredded Parmesan
1/8 teaspoon Smoked Paprika
¼ teaspoon Salt
¼ teaspoon Black Pepper
½ teaspoon Garlic Powder or 2 Fresh Garlic Cloves
2 Tablespoon Fresh Dill, chopped or 1 teaspoon Dried Dill

Directions:

1. Preheat oven to 350F.
2. Place a large pan over medium heat. Add in 1 tablespoon olive oil, spinach, and kale. Cover with a lid and occasionally stir until the greens are wilted.
3. Place the wilted greens in an ice bath for 5 minutes to stop the cooking process.
4. Meanwhile, spray two muffin tins with cooking spray and place one wonton wrapper into each muffin cup. Place in the oven for 10 minutes *(if you do not prebake the wonton wrappers, it will be hard to achieve that crunch you expect from a wonton.)*
5. Next, drain as much liquid from the cooked/chilled greens as possible.
6. In a medium-large bowl, stir together all the filling ingredients until evenly combined.
7. Evenly distribute the filling into all 24 wonton cups. Return to the oven for about 15 minutes until the filling is heated through and the wontons are golden brown.
8. Enjoy!

Macaroni Salad

- **Macaroni Salad**

(Make a day before the party so that the salad can marinate and develop flavor overnight.)

  o Apple Cider Vinegar: A fermented product that contains acetic acid with strands of proteins, enzymes, and healthy bacteria. It results in the chance of weight loss, improving gut health, heart health, skin health, and more.

  o Mayo: Contains unsaturated fats such as omega 3 and 6 fatty acids. It may improve skin, nail, and hair health.

  ▪ **Yield:** About 8 servings. Each serving =1 cup.

Ingredients:

Salad
4 cups Macaroni Noodles, Cooked
1 cup Fresh Red Bell Pepper, small diced
2 *(about 1 cup)* Celery Stalks, small diced, discard *(or save for broth)* white ends
1 cup Red Onion, small diced
8oz Pepper Jack Cheese Block, diced
½ cup Black Olives, Sliced

Dressing
¾ cup Mayo
¼ cup Dill Relish
2 Tablespoons Whole Grain Garlic or Dejon Mustard
1 Teaspoon Granulated Sugar
1 Tablespoon Apple Cider Vinegar
1 Tablespoon Worcestershire Sauce
¼ teaspoon Salt
¼ teaspoon Pepper
1/8 teaspoon Garlic Powder
½ teaspoon Ground Cumin

Garnish *(Optional)*
Sprinkle of Black Sea Salt

Directions:

1. Place a medium pot over high heat filled ¾ way with water. Add in 1 Tablespoon of salt and bring to a boil. Once boiling, stir in a package of macaroni noodles and cook until al dente.
2. Once cooked, drain and rinse the noodles with cold water. Toss with a drizzle of olive oil and place in the fridge to cool.
3. Meanwhile, prep all the other salad ingeminates and place them in a container.
4. In a bowl, whisk together all the dressing ingredients.
5. Add the cooled noodles to the container with the veggies/cheese. Next, pour the dressing on top of the salt mixture and stir until combined.
6. Cover the container with a lid, chill overnight, and enjoy the next day!

- **Fried Goat Cheese with Pesto Sauce**
  - ○ **Pesto:** Packed with antioxidants from both fresh basil and the garlic. Garlic is also great for your digestion, and Olive Oil is a very nutritious oil that may help with weight loss/management.

- **Yield:** About 7 Servings, each person gets 2 pieces

Ingredients:

8oz Goat Cheese, purchase in log form
Vegetable Oil

Dry Batter
½ cup Rice Flour
1 teaspoon Dried Italian Herbs

Wet Batter
½ cup Rice flour
1 Tablespoon Corn Starch
½ teaspoon Baking Powder
½ teaspoon Salt
¼ teaspoon Black Pepper
1 Pinch Cayenne Pepper
½-3/4 cup Club Soda or Water

<u>Chunky Pesto</u>
1 cup Fresh Basil
2 Tablespoons Roasted/Toasted Pine Nuts or any nuts you have on hand
¼, 1 Tablespoon cup Olive oil
2 Tablespoon Water
2 Tablespoons Apple cider vinegar
2 Tablespoons cup Parmesan cheese
1 Roasted Garlic Cloves
Small pinch salt

<u>Garnish Options</u>
Black Sea Salt
Paprika
Balsamic Reduction

Directions:

1. Place all pesto ingredients into a blender and puree until smooth. You may have to stop the blender a couple of times and use a spatula to scrape down the sides/push the basil down to puree properly.
2. If the pesto is warm from the blender, place it in the fridge until ready for it.
3. Fill a deep pot ¾ the way up with Vegetable Oil. Place on the stove over medium-high heat and bring the oil to 350F degrees.
4. Slice ½-inch rounds of goat cheese with a warm/sharp knife. You can dip the knife into hot water between slices if need be.
5. In a bowl, whisk together dry mix. In a separate bowl, whisk together all wet mix ingredients.
6. Once the oil is to temp. Dip the slices of goat cheese into the dry mix, then the wet mixture, and lastly, gently drop into the hot oil.
7. Do not crowd your pot. Only fry 4-6 cheese rounds at a time.
8. Fry each cheese round for about 3 minutes once fried, remove the cheese from the fryer and place it on a paper towel to catch excess grease.
9. Place the cheese on a platter, drizzle with the chilled pesto, and sprinkle with garnish.
10. Enjoy!

Truffle Cheese Chicken Sliders with Micro Greens

- **Truffle Cheese Chicken Sliders with Micro Greens**
  - Truffles: May help reduce inflammation throughout the body, may fight bacterial infections, and may lower cholesterol.
    - **Yield:** 12 Service, 1 Slicer each.

Ingredients:

18-24oz Chicken Breasts
Salt to taste
Fresh Ground Black Pepper to taste
1 Package Fresh Micro Greens or Alfalfa
12 Slider Buns or Rolls

Cheese
2 Tablespoons Sliced Jarred Truffles, small diced. *(If you do not have access to Jarred truffles, you can replace the truffles with roasted peppers)*
8oz block Fresh Sharp White Cheddar, sliced into small chunks
½ Lemon (Fresh Lemon Zest and Juice)
¼ teaspoon Dried Thyme
1/8 teaspoon salt
1/8 teaspoon Black Pepper

Directions:

1. Place a pot of water on the stove and bring to a gentle boil. Place a large enough bowl on top of the pot to create a double boiler.
2. Place all the cheese ingredients in the bowl/double boiler. Stir the cheese mixture occasionally to be fully melted and combined.
3. Remove the truffle cheese from the bowl and pour it into a small square, circle, or rectangle container (spray container with cooking spray). Place the container in the fridge with no cover.
4. Cut the breasts into 12 sections. Each piece of chicken should weigh about 1.5-2oz.
5. Place a pan or cast iron on the stove over medium-high heat. Drizzle one Tablespoon of olive oil into the pan.
6. When the cheese has set/hardened, slice 12 slices of cheese
7. Season the chicken with salt and pepper to taste and place in the pan. Brown each side of the chicken and bring it to an internal temp of 165F.
8. Place a slice of cheese onto each piece of chicken and cover the pan with a lid to melt.
9. Place each piece of chicken onto a bun/cut open roll, and top with microgreens.
10. Enjoy!

My View on Food

From looking at my go-to meals at home, you can see that we do not always eat "healthy," nor do we eat entirely plant-based. Like most families, everyone likes different food items, and it can be challenging if one family member is trying to eat plant-based or on a diet. So, I encourage a wide variety of menu items in my household. With variety, I also like to say is, "I try and balance what I eat out with vegetables and exercise." In order words, I try to incorporate veggies in every meal I eat, even if others in the house do not want them. It is also essential that I stay active at work, go hiking in nature, walk my dogs, and exercise at home.

In my opinion, we as individuals need to keep not only physically healthy but also mentally healthy. I have gone through many mental traumas, and what helps me stay mentally well/happy is my faith, friends, family, food, and exercise.

Plant-Based Vs. Meat Eaters

People eat plant-based for many reasons. Some of those reasons may be for environmental benefits, health benefits, they do not like the taste of meat or dairy, or simply the fact that they love animals and they don't want them to get hurt. There are many types of plant-based diets. Here are the most common below.

- *Vegetarian:* Someone that does not consume any animal flesh (meat, poultry, fish). This person does consume dairy products, but possibly not eggs.
- *Lacto-Ovo:* Someone that does not consume any animal flesh but does eat all dairy products, including eggs (Ovo).
- *Vegan:* Someone that does not consume anything that comes from an animal or any living creature for that matter. Gelatin is made from bone marrow. Lastly, some vegans will not even eat honey because it comes from the living bumblebee.

Types of Meat Eaters:

- *Omnivores/Carnivores:* someone that eats animals' products and plants.

I have full respect for both plant-eaters and meat-eaters. I consider myself to be one of those in-betweeners. By that, I mean sometimes I eat a plant-based meal, and then most of the time, I will eat a meal with meat.

I believe that to have a well-rounded diet (lifestyle of eating), you must consume both meat and plant-based proteins. When you eat both plant-based and meat-based, you can gain a broader amount of essential nutrients needed for your body to function, probably and may help you keep a healthy weight if that is what you are after. Lastly, consuming both plants based and meat-based can help you maintain any chronic illnesses that you may have, like stated throughout this book. However, if you choose one or the other diets, you can still achieve great health benefits depending on the types and quantity of foods you eat daily. I hope you have learned some types from the illnesses and recipes discuss above.

To Diet or Not to Diet?

If you want to lose weight, you cannot just "diet." In my opinion, the word "diet" is very miss used. Diet implies the specific consumption of nutritional foods or supplements to help cure or maintain a sickness, illness, or disease. Diets should not be used to lose weight. Yes, by changing your diet, you may lose weight, but that is not the sole purpose of a diet.

The word diet comes from the Greek word "digital", which means WAY OF LIFE. When you want to go on a diet, it needs to be a lifestyle change to become a healthier person and heal your body through food.

Sources

Happiness, A., Author, & Brewing Happiness. (2020, March 17). Seeded Rye Bread. Retrieved October 19, 2020, from https://www.brewinghappiness.com/seeded-rye-bread/

Alzheimer's Association. (2021). Can Alzheimer's Disease be Prevented? Retrieved May 14, 2021. From https://www.alz.org/alzheimers-dementia/research_progress/prevention

ANAD, (2021, March 3). *Eating Disorder Statistics: General & Diversity Stats: ANAD.* National Association of Anorexia Nervosa and Associated Disorders. https://anad.org/get-informed/about-eating-disorders/eating-disorders-statistics/.

Badaczewski, L. (2020, December 14). *Over the Garden Gate: Permaculture is gardening that imitates nature.* The Times. Retrieved January 27, 2022, from https://www.timesonline.com/story/lifestyle/home-garden/2020/12/14/over-garden-gate-permaculture-gardening-imitates-nature/6521740002/

Cap Wellness Center. (2022). Ask Yourself...What Am I Feeding My Mind? Retrieved January 27, 2022, from http://capwellnesscenter.com/ask-yourself-what-am-i-feeding-my-mind/.

C. (n.d.). (2020) Diet and Nutrition for Energy with COPD. Retrieved November 11, 2020, from https://my.clevelandclinic.org/health/articles/9451-nutritional-guidelines-for-people-with-copd)

Discovery Contribution. (2019, October 22). Common Myths about Eating Disorders Debunked. Center for Discovery, Retrieved May 17, 2021, from https://centerfordiscovery.com/blog/myths-about-eating-disorders/

Group, M. (2021, January 12). Mintel offers global food and DRINKS trends for 2021. Retrieved April 05, 2021, from https://www.nutraceuticalsworld.com/contents/view_breaking-news/2021-01-12/mintel-announces-global-food-and-drinks-trends-for-2021/#:~:text=The%20three%20trends%20announced%20this,Redefined%3B%20and%20United%20by%20Food.&text=In%202021%20and%20beyond%2C%20expect,relief%20activities%2C%20the%20company%20said.

Frazier, Karen. (2021) Alcoholic Drinks for Diabetics. Love to Know, retrieved May 17, 2021, from https://cocktails.lovetoknow.com/cocktail-recipes/alcoholic-drinks-diabetics

Healthline Media a Red Ventures. (2021). 6 Common Types of Eating Disorders and Their Symptoms. Healthline, Retrieved May 17, 2021, from https://www.healthline.com/nutrition/common-eating-disorders#anorexia

Healthline Media a Red Ventures. (2020). The Best Sugar Substitutes for People with Diabetes. Healthline, retrieved May 17, 2021, from https://www.healthline.com/health/type-2-diabetes/diabetes-stevia#stevia

Healthline. (2005-202). Healthline. Retrieved May 25, 2021. Retrieved from https://www.healthline.com.

Sutter health. (2021). Eating Well for Mental Health. Retrieved May 13, 2021, from https://www.sutterhealth.org/health/nutrition/eating-well-for-mental-health

Younkin, L. (2017, December 21). Gout Diet: Foods That Can Help You Control Gout. Retrieved October 23, 2020, from http://www.eatingwell.com/article/290699/gout-diet-foods-that-can-help-you-control-gout/

This picture was taken at a church in Littleton, CO.

Bible Verses And Encouragement

"Man shall not live on bread alone, but on every word that comes from the mouth of God."
~Matthew 4:4

"Be strong and courageous. Do not be afraid; do not be discouraged, for the Lord your God will be with you wherever you go."
~Joshua 1:9

"He Protects us on our journey."
~Joshua 24:17

We will go through many seasons throughout our lifetime. We will come across many unbearable times and many joyous times as well. We must embrace what the Lord gives us and have faith that he is here with us on our journey. We cannot do this on our own. It will all work out in the end.